Nuts & of Self-Publishing

How to Self-Publish Ebooks and Paperbacks

Chris Longmuir

B&J

Published by Barker & Jansen

Copyright © Chris Longmuir, 2017

Cover design by Cathy Helms www.avalongraphics.org

All rights reserved. No part of this publication may be reproduced, stored, or transmitted in any form, or by any means electronic, mechanical or photocopying, recording or otherwise, without the prior permission of the copyright owner.

ISBN: 978-0-9574153-6-2

DEDICATION

This book is dedicated to all those indie authors and publishers who are publishing quality books for discerning readers.

CONTENTS

Introduction

Author's Note

This book has been written using British UK spelling except where it refers to computer terminology. For example, dialog when referring to dialog boxes and program when referring to computer programs.

Introduction

The definition of publishing is the selection, preparation and marketing of printed matter. This has led to the rise of modern-day publishers who do not write the books they publish, instead, they acquire books written by various authors, subject these books to a manufacturing process and supply them to bookstores and retailers. In a nutshell, it could be said that publishers, in the main, do not create the works they turn into books, they copy the work supplied by the authors they contract and change it into something that can be bought and read. A common belief is that there have always been publishers who produce books which we can buy in our favourite bookstore. But this is not the case.

Prior to the fifteenth century and the invention of the printing press, which enabled printed copy to be mass produced, books were prepared by professional copyists on vellum or parchment. Paper became more commonplace after this period and the guilds, which handled the sale of most objects, were involved in the production and sale of books.

In the fifteenth and sixteenth centuries, printers were the people who produced books and performed the roles of editor, publisher and bookseller. The first printer-publisher to produce works in Britain was William Caxton who printed more than ninety books during his lifetime.

Gradually, from the seventeenth century onwards, a new breed of publisher started to emerge, although the publication business was still a mixture of producers and suppliers. It was the nineteenth century which saw the rise of the modern publishers, and the twentieth century when publishers developed into a mammoth book industry which came to dominate publishing.

Over the past century, the belief developed that the only acceptable way to publish a book was by gaining a contract from a well-known publisher. Self-publishing came to be frowned on and references were often made to vanity publishing. This was probably due to the dominance of the market by publishers known as traditional or legacy publishers. Self-publishing was sidelined in order to perpetuate the myth that the only way to publish was by one of these companies.

But self-publishing is not a new thing, nor has it always been associated with vanity. You only have to look at previous self-publishing authors in order to scotch that myth. So, let's do a bit of name-dropping and have a look at who, in the past, has self-published.

William Blake, the famed English poet and painter self-published some of his best-known works. Jane Austen paid Thomas Egerton to publish Sense and Sensibility. Hogarth Press was established by Virginia Woolf and her husband for the purpose of publishing her books. Many other authors, whose names are easily recognized, include; Margaret Atwood, Elizabeth Barrett Browning, Lord Byron, Alexander Dumas, Thomas Hardy, Ernest Hemingway, Stephen King, Rudyard Kipling, Edgar Allan Poe, Beatrix Potter, George Bernard Shaw, and John Grisham, and these are only a few.

Self-publishing is currently going through a time of change and although there are still some who subscribe to the myths, these are gradually being exposed. After all, publishing only became a business following the rise of companies prepared to invest in authors in order to profit from their work. When an author decides to self-publish it changes that dynamic.

Encouraged by the rise of electronic publishing and the ease of publishing books to this market, self-publishing has been resurrected, and many authors, whether they are experienced or not, have seized this opportunity to make their books available. This book deals with the phenomena of self-publishing as it is today.

As the book progresses it will take you through the stages of self-publishing, from the initial decision to the actual process of publication with step-by-step guides. It will examine the advantages and disadvantages and help you avoid some of the pitfalls along the way.

Self-publishing is not difficult once you have the roadmap and know what is expected and what you are doing. I wish you well on your journey to self-publication.

1

Is Self-Publishing for You?

The holy grail for most writers is finding a publisher, and there's nothing wrong with that.

However, except for a fortunate few, the search for a publisher can take years, and when you are lucky enough to find one, if indeed you do, it can take between one to two years for the publishing process before you see your book on sale.

There are some self-published writers who have nothing good to say about traditional publishing in the same way that there are traditionally published writers who despise the self-publishing route. But publishing is changing and there is room for all kinds of publishing models, and only you can decide which model to pursue. My task in this book is to provide you with information about the self-publishing route should you decide this is the best option for you.

I have been self-publishing books since 2011, initially ebooks and then paperbacks. When I started out I had a lot of enthusiasm and very little experience and I had to learn the hard way, by trial and error. I read a lot and researched a lot, building up my expertise as I went along, and now I find that my advice is often sought by those authors setting out on the path to self-publication.

This book is based on my Nuts and Bolts of Self-Publishing workshop and I hope that by sharing my knowledge and experience with you I will help you to avoid some of the problems you might encounter. Self-publishing your own books can be hard work as well as an immensely satisfying experience but if you can think about it as the business part of authorship you won't go wrong.

I find the term self-published can be a bit of a catch-all, meaning different things to different people. However, even though self-publishing was often the norm before the rise of modern publishers, during the last century the derogatory term of 'vanity' became attached to it. An author who aspired to publication but could not attract a publisher and resorted to publishing a book themselves was deemed to be 'vain'. This was a misnomer because as soon as they attracted a publisher they were no longer 'vain'. And who would dare suggest vanity in the same breath as some of the self-publishers I mentioned in the introduction. I could mention a lot more but in the interests of getting down to the nuts and bolts of self-publishing, I won't.

Before we start it is important to understand that there are different types of self-publishers, just as there are different types of traditional publishers.

In recent years the rise of indie authors and publishers has become an acceptable part of the publishing world. These are the authors and small publishers who have embraced the self-publishing ethos through the publication of electronic books and print on demand paperbacks. They operate professionally and produce quality books.

When the indie label is adopted by writers who operate less professionally this can create confusion and in some cases devalue the books indie publishers and authors are producing. So, this might be the place to examine the role of the indie.

2

What is an Indie?

The indie

Indie is short for independent. Indie authors are writers who are bypassing traditional publishers and are publishing their books independently.

They are responsible for everything from the initial writing through to the sale of the finished product.

The indie author, by default, also becomes an indie publisher, although the indie label also applies to small independent publishers with one or more authors. The books produced by the indie author or publisher are not part of mainstream publishing by major companies whose names are household words. You know the ones I mean, Penguin, Harper Collins, Macmillan, and the others.

The name 'indie' was not coined by self-publishing authors, it has earlier connections with the music industry and with films. But it has the same meaning, something that is independently produced. I am not aware of when it started to be used for books and literature which were previously referred to as self-published, but the name seems appropriate.

I have looked at various definitions of indie, and it always comes back to something produced by an independent artist, studio, producer, writer, company, or group, which is not affiliated with a larger or more commercial organization. In the case of literature, it is a book published outside of mainstream publishing.

In an article, at CNN.com (Cable News Network), journalist Catherine Andrews wrote: "The term 'indie' traditionally refers to independent art – music, film, literature or anything that fits under the broad banner of culture – created outside of the mainstream and without corporate financing."

So, indie authors are writers who self-publish their books. Those authors who tackle the task in a professional way often produce books which are indistinguishable from those distributed by traditional publishers. I admit, however, there are some self-published books that should never have been published, but it is relatively easy to separate those from the well-written ones by checking the quality with the 'Look Inside' and the 'Try a Sample' features on Amazon.

But I am sure you are wondering why a writer would choose to be an indie? Why go through all the hassle of independently publishing your book when there may be publishers ready and willing to publish it for you? Before I tackle that issue, perhaps you would like to see what options an author has to attain publication.

3

Publishing Options

The author has completed the book, has had it edited and proofread, it is as good as it can be, and it is ready for publication. What are the options?

1. Traditional publisher

The traditional or legacy publisher is often the first choice. How hard can it be?

The author who chooses to follow this route starts off on a merry-go-round of submissions and rejections from publishers. The next line of attack is often trying to find an agent which leads to more submissions and rejections.

You may think this only applies to new authors, those who have never published before, but I am afraid it is exactly the same for authors with a track record who are not currently under contract to a publisher. Representation by an agent is probably the only advantage an established author may have over a new author.

The outcome is often the same. This is because publishers are in business to sell books, and the publication of a book is simply a means to that end. This is why you see so many celebrity biographies and cookbooks on the bookstore shelves. However, if the publisher thinks your book will sell in the millions then you may get that elusive contract, although a friend of mine in the publishing industry informed me most first novels sell fewer than 300 copies.

In financial terms, royalties are paid at the rate of anything between 7.5% to 10% for paperbacks. Many publishers give the author an advance payment, but this is an advance of royalties, it is not a payment for writing the book. If for example, £1,000 is given before publication of the book no royalties will be paid until they exceed the amount of the advance.

2. Small press

If the author has been unable to interest a traditional publisher there are always the small presses, the small publishers, and the independents.

The chances of acceptance may be greater here, but small presses and publishers have small budgets to match, so may be restricted in what they can take on.

Small publishers rarely pay royalty advances. On the other hand, some of them offer higher royalties. However, I have noticed some of them price their books higher than their bigger brothers, the traditional publishers, which makes the books they publish less competitive in a crowded market.

Small presses often use the same service suppliers and distributors as the self-publishers. The main benefit for the author, if they publish this way, is that they do not have to do everything themselves. However, marketing and distribution may be less than that provided by a larger publishing house.

The new author also needs to be aware that a major disadvantage when seeking publication by a small press is the number of vanity publishers masquerading as small publishers. Unlike the traditional and small press publishers, the vanity publisher will expect the author to pay a substantial fee for publication.

This makes it essential for the author to research a small press before signing a contract.

3. Self-publish

Self-publishing has developed a bad press over the years and there is still a stigma attached to it, although that is gradually lessening.

However, this is not helped by the fact that this method of publishing includes the vanity publishers as well as the indies.

A vanity publisher, not to be confused with reputable firms offering author services, will promise everything and will charge accordingly. They are in the business of selling publishing services to authors. They are unconcerned about the content or quality of the writing and will promise to distribute the books after they are published, but in most cases do not do this. The only person they distribute to is the author.

With self-publishing, the author outsources the services provided by a traditional publisher and has to cover the costs for editing, cover art, and formatting themselves.

Alternatively, they can buy a package from a company offering author services, bearing in mind the risks involved from the vanity press masquerading as author services providers.

Some print on demand firms also charge a small setup fee, and if the author is unwilling to outsource services because they prefer everything to be done for them, there are reputable printing or publishing companies who can provide this. The services required must be paid for but there should be no fee attached to the actual publication apart from initial setup fees and the cost of author copies of the book. If a publishing company demands a substantial amount to publish, then the chances are the author has fallen foul of a vanity publisher.

There are various ways to self-publish. For example, Amazon's Kindle Direct Publishing, IngramSpark, FeedaRead, and Lulu.com, are reputable self-publishing firms who use print on demand and I am sure there are others. But care should be taken to ensure they are genuine. Always check a publisher's credentials on such sites as Preditors and Editors at pred-ed.com, and Writer Beware at sfwa.org.

A useful guide, compiled by the Watchdog team at the Alliance of Independent Authors (ALLi) is free to ALLi members but is also available for purchase online. *How to Choose A Self-Publishing Service 2016: A Writer's Guide from the Alliance of Independent Authors* (updated every year) is a mine of information. It lists many of the companies providing author services, indicating costs and what you can expect for the money. It details which companies provide the best services as well as those to be wary of. In my view, this guide is essential reading for the author considering buying services rather than taking the do-it-yourself approach.

4. Print on demand (POD)

Gone are the days when an author who self-published had to store thousands of books in their garage or spare bedroom because the only way to acquire their books was through a print run. Modern methods of printing mean that each book can be printed when it is required.

The costs involved are the print costs, and if dealing with a local printer these can be negotiated. Of course, there is more work involved in formatting, providing a book cover etc, but this work can be outsourced if necessary. With POD each copy of a book costs more than copies supplied by a large print run, but although a print run can be cheaper there is the temptation to order too many copies to keep the price down. This can lead to storage problems and unsold books.

5. Electronic

Publishing an ebook is relatively simple and is cost free if everything is done by the author. However, it is better to outsource the editing, the proofreading and the book cover. The formatting can also be outsourced if the author is technologically challenged, although it is comparatively easy to do with a modicum of time and patience. Once initial expenses are accounted for there is no further outlay.

Financially, ebook royalties for the self-publishing indie author range between 35% to 85%, depending on the distributor and the price of the ebook.

By comparison, mainstream publishers pay anything between 17.5% and 20% royalties to the traditionally published author when they publish their books as ebooks.

Reasons why authors choose to publish independently

The answer is, of course, in the heading.

The main reason an author becomes an indie is because it makes them truly independent. They make their own decisions and pay all the bills associated with publishing their books. However, authors may take various routes to get there before they make up their minds that this is the path to publication they wish to take.

Perhaps it would be helpful to look at some of the things that can affect that decision.

1. The author is tired of being knocked back by publishers and agents, and disillusioned by constant rejections. So they decide to go it alone.

Many people associate this with failure and the self-publishing stigma can kick in, labelling the authors as 'wannabes' who have been unable to attain success elsewhere. This is doing a disservice to most of the writers who choose to self-publish, and it is worth bearing in mind that many of them are not new to writing. A substantial number of them are professional authors with a wealth of experience who have previously published using traditional means.

2. Lost contracts

Due to the changing publishing scene and the economic climate, many mid-list authors are losing their contracts. Some of these authors have been with the same publisher for years and now find themselves no longer wanted.

3. The backlist

Prolific authors with many published books now out of print, and where the publishing rights have reverted to the author, are giving their books a new lease of life as ebooks.

4. Making money

Some writers, especially the ones new to publishing, become indie authors and publishers because they believe all authors make oodles of money. They read the media releases about indie writers striking it big and making millions. They read about Fifty Shades of Grey, and authors such as John Locke, and Amanda Hocking, and think it is easy.

However, the sad truth is writers and authors, in general, do not make a lot of money, and the majority do not make a living wage.

5. They want to attract a publisher

Stories abound, particularly on the internet, that the big publishers are using indie books as their new slush pile and are cherry picking authors who appear to be selling an inordinate number of ebooks. I do not know whether this is true, but I do know a small number of authors have acquired contracts this way. Notice, I said a few, not thousands. So, some writers think by becoming indie authors they will be discovered. I wish them luck.

6. *Independence and control*

I have left this reason until last because it is the reason I am an indie. As I said previously, indie is short for independent, and I am a very independent person. The writers in this group want to control the whole process themselves. They want to be the ones deciding what to write and when to write it. But they must embrace the business side of the venture as well as the writing, not forgetting the hassle of marketing, distribution and promotion. However, the thing I love most about being an indie is the freedom it provides.

4

Self-Publishing

Before I go into detail about the processes of self-publishing I thought it would be useful to summarize what is involved. So, here it is, in a nutshell.

What you have to do:

1. Write the best book you can.

2. Revise and rewrite – make it better.

3. Edit and proofread – make it even better.

4. Outsource an editor, the more polished the book the less it will cost.

5. Outsource the cover.

6. Write the blurb.

7. Acquire ISBNs for print books, not necessary for Kindle ebooks.

8. Format the manuscript for electronic publishing.

9. Format the manuscript for print publishing.

10. Create publishing accounts – electronic and POD (Print on Demand).

11. Promote your book.

12. Write the next book.

Self-publishing

A traditionally published author has one role, and that is to write books.

A self-published author has three roles; author, publisher, business person.

If you self-publish your book you are a publisher and you have to take on all the tasks that are supplied to authors by traditional publishers. So, once you have written the best book possible you need to factor in editing, proofing, cover, blurb, and distribution.

Apart from that, you are running a business, which means all the admin tasks, bookkeeping, accounting etc are your responsibility.

Editors

Editors, like writers, come in many guises. Just as there are writers who publish books riddled with errors, there are also editors who have no other credentials except they read books, so you need to take care in your choice of editor.

1. Check their credentials.
2. How much experience they have.
3. Can they supply references from other authors, and don't take it on the editor's word only. It is your book, you are entitled to check who you employ to work on it.
4. Seek advice from other authors.
5. Seek recommendations from professional organizations like ALLi (Alliance of Independent Authors), or Reedsy at reedsy.com who have a database of editors.

I will go into more detail later in the book. In the meantime, I want to consider the rise of electronic publishing which has opened the door to many aspiring authors in search of publication.

5

Ebooks and eReaders

An ebook is the easiest, best, and most profitable way for authors to self-publish. So, before looking at how to do this I will provide you with some information about ebooks and eReaders.

Ebooks and eReaders

The changing perception of self-publishing came about because of the rise of ebooks and eReaders.

More and more people are turning to ebooks but there are still many who think ebooks belong to the technological age and are not like the books they have been accustomed to in the past.

So, despite the many readers who have embraced new electronic ways of reading, others are convinced that nothing can replace print books.

In simple terms, the ebook is a digital or electronic book. It is a file that is computer generated and is read on a computer screen or a handheld device such as an eReader or iPad.

There is an unfortunate spin-off from this because the person who buys the ebook may not see it as a product requiring payment. A paper book is a physical thing as is the eReader to which the ebook is downloaded, but the ebook can appear to be simply words that appear on the eReader. As a result, many people expect all ebooks to be free in the same way many internet downloads are free.

However, the publication of the ebook file does have a cost. The writer has spent time writing the words contained within the file, and it may have taken a year or longer to complete the book or novel. It also has the normal start up costs that print books have; for example, payment for the cover art, the illustrator, the editor, and the formatting. The advantage an ebook has over a print book is the saving on printing, storage and distribution costs. This is the reason ebooks can be sold at a cheaper price than a comparable print book.

A print book can be bought from a bookstore, a supermarket, or the internet, from a variety of stores such as Amazon, Barnes and Noble, and Waterstones. An ebook requires to be downloaded from an online store including the ones already mentioned. To read the ebook it requires a screen, which can be a computer screen, a tablet such as the iPad, or a dedicated eReader.

An eReader is designed specifically for the purpose of reading digital ebooks and publications. It is a mobile electronic device much the same size and shape as a physical print book. The advantage it has over the print book is its portability. It is lighter than a print book and can contain many thousands of books which are available to read at the touch of a button. Most models have wireless connectivity with a direct link to an online ebook store, which means an ebook can be bought at any time and be immediately available. There is no need to wait for a bookstore to open, or make the journey to buy a book. It is ideal for travellers, although many people have come to prefer their electronic eReader to a print book, to be read at any time. Others read both.

Another advantage ebooks and eReaders have is the ability to adjust the size of text, something you cannot do with a print book. This is helpful for those readers whose vision is not perfect. Likewise, the eReader is easier to hold than a print book because it does not require pages to be held open.

There are different makes of eReader and they do not all use the same type of files, although most ebooks are published in file formats compatible with the different models of eReaders.

However, because of the varying file formats, what can be read on one make of eReader may not necessarily be readable on another.

For example, Amazon's Kindle uses its own mobi file format, these files can only be read on a Kindle. Many other eReaders use the epub file format which is readable on most of the other makes of eReader, such as Kobo or Nook. An epub file cannot be read on a Kindle.

Because of this variation in file formats, the buyer would be advised to use the store associated with their eReader to ensure they will be able to read the ebook they order. More knowledgeable buyers who are aware of which file format is compatible with their eReader, have the ability to shop around.

Then there is DRM (Digital Rights Management) which encrypts ebooks so they can only be read on the device belonging to the buyer. Some ebook sellers insist that the ebooks they sell are DRM protected, others do not. Amazon, for example, makes DRM encryption optional for Kindle ebooks.

Ereaders continue to develop, and some of the latest models have more resemblance to tablet computers. These include the Apple iPad, the Kindle Fire, and various android tablets. The difference between them and the original eReader is the screen.

The dedicated eReaders, such as Amazon's Kindle (not the Kindle Fire), Barnes and Noble's Nook, W H Smith's Kobo, and the Sony Reader, use an electronic paper technology called e-ink. Reading from screens using this type of display is easier on the eye; the text is displayed as black print on a white or cream background which makes it similar to reading a printed page. There is no glare on the screen from sunlight and, similar to a print book, the ebook can be read in any lighting condition apart from the dark, although newer models are now backlit which makes reading in the dark possible.

The newer tablet models have full colour, they can be used for other activities as well as reading, such as games, music, video, emails, and browsing the internet. However, the screens are reflective and they do not use the e-ink display. The outcome is that they are less easy on the eye, and are impossible to read in sunlight.

History of ebooks and eReaders

The rapid increase in the sales of ebooks and eReaders over the past few years gives the impression that this technology is new and is a twenty-first-century development.

Nothing could be further from the truth.

Project Gutenberg was launched in 1971. This was the year they digitized the United States Declaration of Independence, making it the first ebook in the world. The aim of this voluntary project is to digitize all books which are no longer in copyright in order to preserve them for future generations. Volunteers retype and scan the out-of-copyright texts. Books by Jane Austen, Charlotte Bronte, Sir Arthur Conan Doyle, H G Wells, and a host of others can be found on the Project Gutenberg website for free download. And from a small start with one book in 1971 the project has grown and now contains over 50,000 free books, most of them classics.

However, it was the 1990s before the development of ebook publication started to progress. In 1991 the Project Gutenberg began to take its present form, and the target at that time was to digitize one book each month. By 1996 it was a book a day, and today about 400 books are added each month. Then, in 1993, Digital Book Inc. produced the first fifty digital books on floppy disc.

The way in which people read ebooks has also progressed over the years. In the early days, ebooks were read on computers, and software was produced to enable the ebook to be read in a similar fashion to a traditional book.

The most popular reading software at the time was the Adobe Reader, launched in 1993, and Microsoft Reader, in 2000. Both these computer-based readers are still available, and Adobe Reader, now known as Acrobat Reader, is widely used to read

PDF (portable document format) files, although Microsoft Reader is not so popular.

An early ebook was a Stephen King novella, *Riding the Bullet*, which was published in 2000 in digital form to be read on a computer. I have been unable to determine which reading software the ebook used but I suspect it was Microsoft Reader which was launched in the same year the novella was published. It is estimated that 400,000 copies were downloaded in the first hour causing many computers to crash.

A variety of portable devices were appearing on the market as early as 1998 when the Rocket eBook and the Softbook were launched. These were the predecessors of the eReaders available today, but their capacity was far less. Instead of the thousands of ebooks the modern versions can hold, these early eReaders struggled to contain 10 books. Over the years, eReaders continued to develop culminating in the ones we have today.

The Sony Reader was the first to be launched in Britain in 2008, although it had been on sale in the US since 2006. This was followed soon after by Amazon's Kindle in 2007 in the US, although it was not available in the UK until 2009. Other popular eReaders were slower to appear in the UK, with W H Smith introducing the Kobo Reader in their stores in 2011, while Barnes and Noble introduced their Nook Reader to the UK in 2012.

Ebooks versus print books

Ebooks and eReaders have gained popularity over the last few years and, while many readers will not forsake the printed book, the numbers reading ebooks have increased substantially.

Statistics indicate that, in the US, the revenue from sales of ebooks grew from $64 million to $3,042 million between 2008 to 2012, and the number of actual ebooks sold increased from 10 million to 457 million over the same period. That is a massive increase. However, it does not tell the full story because the statistics are compiled by the AAP (Association of

American Publishers) and the figures are obtained through Bowker, the ISBN book registering agency in the US. Many indie ebooks are not registered with an ISBN because ebooks sold by Amazon for the Kindle do not require one. Therefore, it is logical to assume that the figures are grossly underestimated and the sales of ebooks are far greater.

The following statistics originated from Amazon in relation to Kindle Direct Publishing which is where many indie authors publish their ebooks: *"more than a thousand KDP authors now each sell more than a thousand copies a month, some have already reached hundreds of thousands of sales, and two have already joined the Kindle Million Club."*

The Million Club is for authors who have sold a million ebooks. There are only fourteen authors in this club to date, and the two indie authors who qualify for the Million Club are John Locke and Amanda Hocking. The others are the bestselling authors Lee Child, Nora Roberts, George R R Martin, Charlaine Harris, James Patterson, Janet Evanovich, Stieg Larsson, Michael Connolly, David Baldacci, Suzanne Colins, Kathryn Stockett, and Stephanie Meyer.

To have obtained such a large share of the book buying market over a relatively short time indicates that ebooks are providing a satisfying reading experience. The number of sales indicated by the indie author publishing platform KDP (Kindle Direct Publishing) confirms my belief that there are many quality indie ebooks available.

The indie ebook

It is said that one of the advantages of e-publishing is that 'anyone can publish a book,' and one of the disadvantages is that 'anyone can publish a book'.

I think this illustrates the current e-publishing situation. There are multiple well-written, well edited and formatted ebooks available, but likewise, the reverse can be true.

There is no excuse for badly written, and badly edited books, although formatting comes into a different category. Some well-written books are let down by bad formatting, however, this is not exclusive to indie ebooks. Many traditionally published ebooks suffer from formatting glitches as well. I think that may be due to some publishers using their print files to publish ebooks. When publishing a print book the format used is PDF (portable document format), this is a fixed format and once the print is placed on the page it does not move. Ebooks, however, require a format which makes the print flow from line to line in accordance with the size of the font in order to maintain the readability of the page on a screen.

Apart from this, a book that is perfectly laid out may inexplicably develop irregularities in the formatting due to the conversion process. This can replace symbols for certain letters, particularly noticeable in some traditionally published books where the conversions have been made using layouts for hardbacks and paperbacks. Another reason for these formatting glitches could be incompatible fonts. The conversion process prefers simple fonts such as Times New Roman.

The indie ebook is perhaps less prone to this type of formatting glitch because indie books generally appear as ebooks first, and the formatting is specific to electronic publishing. Nevertheless, the conversion process can still throw up errors and books with tables or diagrams do not always convert well.

6

Ebooks or Paperbacks

It is possible for a self-publishing author to publish hardback editions but very few do. The majority who choose to self-publish do so in paperback or as an ebook or a combination of both. The choice is yours to make.

Over recent years the paperback has replaced the hardback as the traditional way to read, and writers and readers associate books with the printed version. For this reason, it is not surprising that the self-publisher yearns to hold their very own paperback in their hands and to see it on bookstore shelves. And I must admit this experience is one we all aspire to, even the most ardent digital publisher. But time marches on and, regretfully, books are no longer the sole preserve of bookstores and libraries. Online bookstores proliferate offering a larger selection of books, both digital and paperback, than any High Street bookstore could ever offer.

Ebooks, as I explained in the previous chapter, have been around longer than we think, but it is only over the past ten years that they have risen to prominence, and their popularity has increased over the past five or six years.

In my experience, readers are now divided into three groups: the hard-core of ardent print fans who would never consider reading an ebook; the readers who read both print and digital depending on their location; and readers who have completely embraced digital books in the form of ebooks, iBooks or audio books.

Authors planning to self-publish would be wise to consider the digital option as well as the more traditional option.

One of the main reasons for self-publishing digitally is money. You will have an initial outlay for editing, formatting, and cover design, but once those costs are met there are no further expenses unless you decide to pay for advertising and promotion.

With print books, you will have the same initial outlay, but there will also be continuing costs for printing and shipping. Of course, any promotion or marketing cost, such as adverts, will apply to both digital and print versions.

Your share of an ebook's profits is also larger than that of print books. For an Amazon Kindle ebook, it will be either 35% or 70%, depending on your selling price. An ebook priced at £3.99 will provide a better monetary return than the same print book priced at £9.99 due to the recurring production costs for the latter.

The author also has more control over the selling price of their book. They can set the price and vary it at the touch of a button. However, Amazon's print on demand service KDP (Kindle Direct Publishing) has a minimum price rate for paperbacks and does not allow you to select a free option for ebooks.

Changes and revisions can be made easily. For example, if you find a misspelling that has slipped through, it is easy to rectify. The digital ebook will remain on sale while the amendments are taking place, but the print book will be removed from sale until the republishing process has been completed. This can vary from a few days to a week, although the book is still featured on Amazon.

Digital ebooks have a benefit for readers as well because they are immediately available after purchase, and they do not have to wait for delivery or a trip to the bookstore or library before they start reading.

Another very real benefit for the author who self-publishes is the availability of reports which tell you exactly how many books or ebooks you have sold. Instead of waiting for a yearly or half-yearly royalty statement from your publisher which is written in such a way you still might not know how much you have earned from the sales of your books, a self-publisher can access this information on a daily basis.

Something that should be considered if you are still pursuing the dream of that traditional deal, is that digital books never go out of print, therefore you would be advised to scrutinize contracts carefully as well as seeking professional advice. Within the UK the Society of Authors provides a free contract vetting service.

7

Designing Your Book

The design of your book is a major factor for the self-publisher. It is important for both electronic books and paperbacks. The ebook has to look good on the Amazon product page, therefore the cover must be attractive and the description must be written in a way to entice readers to buy your book.

Likewise, the paperback must be designed in such a way that it will be comparable to any other book on the bookstore shelves, and should not stick out as being different and therefore self-published.

In the main, readers are not concerned with who publishes a book. They do not walk into a bookstore and demand a book published by Penguin, or any of the other major publishers, but they may demand a book written by Stephen King, or even Chris Longmuir. However, they do expect their books to look like every other book in relation to size and attractive cover design and blurb, and anything that looks different can build resistance in the buyer.

There are several elements that go into the design of your book to make it look attractive and worth buying. They are:-

1. The book cover;

2. The front matter;

3. The body of the book (the text);

4. The back matter.

The book cover

The book cover of an ebook is simply the front cover image, there is no need for a back cover. The image, either JPEG or PNG, should be good quality, at least 72 dots per inch (DPI), and the ideal measurement is 2,500 x 1600 pixels.

The book cover of a print book contains a front cover, a back cover, and a spine.

The front cover features an illustration suited to the content of the book, the title, subtitle (if any), and author. It can also include a 'puff', this is a quote provided by an appropriate person, such as a well-known author.

The spine features the book title and author name.

The back cover of the book features the blurb, author information (optional), cover design information, the ISBN, the bar code, and the price of the book.

Many self-publishers do not include a price on the back cover thinking this gives them the flexibility to change prices. This is a fallacy because the price is usually encoded in the bar code, therefore to change the price it would be necessary to change the bar code unless the author does not intend to distribute to bookstores. Omitting the price also has the effect of making the book look different to all the other books on sale. It might also make a potential buyer replace it on the bookstore shelf rather than ask the price.

A professionally designed book cover submitted as a PDF is a must. Of course, you can design your own cover but few of us have access to the special fonts which cover illustrators use, nor do we have their expertise in design, and you do not want to have your book stand out as amateurish.

A Google search will reveal many book cover designers, some reasonably priced, some not. And some do special starving author rates! The important thing is to look at the covers they have previously done and decide whether they suit the type of book you have written.

The blurb

This is what goes on your back cover and it is a very difficult thing to achieve. Compiling a blurb is a copyrighting skill, not the kind of skill it takes to write a book. Think advertising, not synopsis. It needs to be short and punchy and should indicate the genre and the main character, plus why a reader would want to invest in this book. If you put a synopsis on the back they know the story, so why would they need to buy the book?

Front matter

These are the pages at the beginning of the book before the story starts. A reader may not pay too much attention to them unless they look different and out of place. In the paperback version of your book these pages should include:-

1. Half Title: This is the first page of the book. It contains the title of the book and nothing else, the back or verso of this page is blank unless it is used for a frontispiece (sometimes these two pages are not included for economic reasons).

2. Frontispiece: This is optional. It is the photograph or illustration on the verso, or back of the half title page.

3. Title Page: This page contains the title of the book, the subtitle (if any), the author's name under the title, and the publisher's name, usually at the bottom of the page.

4. Copyright page: This goes on the back or verso of the title page and contains a copyright statement, a legal statement, the ISBN number, publication date, cataloguing information, and various credits. The font on this page is usually smaller than the font used throughout the rest of the book.

5. Dedication: Again, this is optional, but if you wish to include one it comes on the page immediately after, and facing the copyright page. The verso of this page is usually blank.

6. Table of Contents: This comes next and is most commonly used in nonfiction books such as this one. It is not usually included in print editions of fictional books unless the chapters have headings. However, it is often to be seen as a list of chapter numbers in ebooks which I find intensely annoying.

7. Acknowledgements: This is where an author expresses thanks for any help received during the writing of the book.

Other things included in the front matter might be lists of figures, tables, or illustrations, or an introduction, preface, or foreword. It all depends on the type of book you wish to publish, and the best advice I can give is to look at how other similar books are laid out. Study where things are placed on the page and elsewhere, and importantly, the different fonts used in respect of different pages, for example, the copyright page is often published in a smaller font than the rest of the front matter, while the title uses a larger more prominent font.

In the electronic version of your book, the front matter can be cut back to the basics. You will, of course, need the title of the book and the author's name, plus a copyright statement and a TOC (table of contents).

Body of your book

This comes after the front matter and is the work, fiction or nonfiction, which you have been slaving over for weeks, months, or years.

Your first chapter should start on a right-hand page and the following chapters should always start on a new page. They should be formatted so that they do not start at the top of the page, except in the case of ebooks where too much space often results in a blank page. It is up to the author how much blank space is left before the start of the chapter, bearing in mind that too much might result in a longer book and therefore a greater printing expense. For the same reason, it is wasted space to start every chapter, except for the first one, on the right-hand page and the majority of published books no longer follow this tradition.

Page lengths in the print version should be uniform, therefore the widows and orphans option in your word processing software should be turned off. And once you have received your proof copy it is worth checking if the end of a sentence containing only a few words has carried forward to a new page at the end of the chapter. This is easily rectified by a bit of judicious editing eg the removal of a few words. Attention to this kind of detail will ensure your book looks professional.

Back matter

This is where you put all the other material that was not included in the front matter. It is not essential to have back matter but the addition of some does add to the professional look. In fiction, this is where you can put your author biography a section named 'About the Author'. A list of your previous publications could also be included here.

If your book requires an index, a glossary, an appendix, a bibliography, endnotes or notes, a list of contributors, copyright permissions, or anything else that does not fit elsewhere, this is the place to put it.

Again, similar to my advice on the front matter, check other published books and pay attention to the fonts and layout of these sections. It will make all the difference to the look of your book.

8

Publishing an Ebook

You can publish your book to digital platforms in a variety of ways.

The most popular platform is Amazon's KDP (Kindle Direct Publishing) and the process is relatively easy once you have formatted your file. More of this later.

The file you upload can be either a Microsoft Word or HTML document. The same Microsoft Word file can be edited to meet Smashwords requirements and after upload, provided it meets the requirements for their Premium catalogue, Smashwords will distribute it to all the major online ebook sellers. This is by far the easiest way.

Some authors, however, prefer to upload their ebooks to each online seller themselves and the major ebook retailers will provide the tools to enable you to do this. Leaving KDP out of the equation, the other main online sellers are:-

i) Apple iBooks, their ebook design program, iBooks Author is a free download. This program also has the ability to create animations, video content, and interactive 3D books. However, the software is only available for Apple Mac computers.

ii) Kobo Writing Life at kobo.com is the platform where you upload your file for them to convert into an ebook.

iii) Barnes and Noble, use Nook Press at nookpress.com. This is an online self-publishing website for ebooks and print. However, several reputable internet sites indicate that Nook Press uses Author Solutions, a company which has many critics. Therefore caution is advised.

The best guide to formatting ebooks is the *Smashwords Style Guide* by Mark Coker which is free. You can get it on the Smashwords website or from Amazon.

In order to publish to Kindle, you upload your Word file to KDP (Kindle Direct Publishing) at kdp.amazon.com but it is important that your file does not have any autoformat or autocorrect options switched on, nor should it have tabs or indents made with the space bar as these can cause havoc with the conversion process. I advise consulting the above Smashwords guide.

For distribution to other ebook sellers eg Kobo, Barnes and Noble, Apple iBooks etc, I use Smashwords at smashwords.com, although I understand D2D (Draft2Digital) at draft2digital.com is also a good option.

It is important to note that if you sign up to the Kindle Select option with KDP you must agree that your ebook will be exclusive to Amazon and cannot be on sale with any other seller.

Ebook royalties

Royalty is the wrong terminology because a royalty is what a publisher pays you as your share of book sales, but it is an easily understood description of your share of the sale which is the reason I use it.

If you price your book on KDP for less than £1.99/$2.99 or more than £9.99/$9.99 you will receive 35% as your share. However, if you price your book anywhere between £1.99/$2.99 and £9.99/$9.99 your share will be 70%.

Selling your ebook

Where you sell your ebook is dependent on whether you have

chosen the KDP Select option that Amazon offers. If you choose this option you make your ebook exclusive to Amazon Kindle. You cannot go wider, you cannot publish to Smashwords, iBooks or anywhere else. Effectively, you have given Amazon the exclusive right to sell and distribute your book, and the agreement you make with Amazon states: *"During this period of exclusivity, you cannot sell or distribute, or give anyone else the right to sell or distribute, your Digital Book (or a book that is substantially similar), in digital format in any territory where you have rights."* This exclusive deal means you cannot even publish parts of your book on your own website, nor can you sell or give away copies of your ebook.

The advantages of being in KDP Select are exclusive opportunities to take part in discounting deals and free book promotions, plus inclusion in the Kindle Unlimited lending library where you are paid in accordance with how many pages have been read. The current rate for the number of pages read at the time of writing this is $0.00411 per page.

The disadvantages of exclusivity with Amazon by opting for KDP Select is the inability to sell in other markets. No doubt, Amazon has the largest digital book market share, particularly in the US and the UK, but that is changing, particularly with the growth of the Apple iPad and the availability of iBooks worldwide. Amazon may currently be the major player when it comes to the sale of ebooks, but the market for iBooks is growing fast, and it is interesting to note that while Amazon sells in 12 territories, Apple sells in 51 countries.

An obvious place to sell your ebook is from your own website, and while that may have been a profitable pursuit a year or so ago, it is now fraught with difficulties. The reason for this is the EU legislation enacted on 1st January 2015 which applied VAT (Value Added Tax) on all digital products, including ebooks, sold in the European Union.

The changes brought in meant that VAT was no longer applied in the seller's country, it was incurred in the buyer's country on each sale made, even if it was only a single ebook.

For example, if you sell one copy of your ebook to someone in Germany, then the German rate of VAT applies, and the VAT charged has to be remitted to the country where the sale was made. You also have to register for VAT with each country where you have sales.

These changes have made selling to the EU a nightmare because each country has a different rate of VAT which ranges from the Luxembourg rate of 17% to the Swedish rate of 25%.

As a matter of interest, the VAT rate in Germany is 19%, Spain 21%, and in France 20%.

One of the difficulties is knowing how to price your ebook because the EU has made it a legal requirement to display the price of your book prior to the purchase being made. You may not know which country the buyer is in, so how do you know the VAT rate and what price to charge?

One way to avoid this complication is to round the charges to the UK VAT rate of 20% for selling purposes, but you will still be required to remit the correct rate of VAT to the country concerned, which means you gain on some sales and lose out on others.

The registration situation, however, is not so dire as it could be if you had to deal with all the EU countries yourself because, in the UK, you can register voluntarily for VAT with HMRC to become part of the VAT Mini One Stop Shop (VAT MOSS) to report and pay VAT due on sales of digital services in the EU. However, the quarterly returns you make have to be itemized for every sale, including the VAT due to the specific countries. So, although the actual payment of VAT to the countries concerned has been taken care of, it is still an administrative nightmare.

However, there have been minor changes made in respect of the VAT regulations due to the work of various lobbying groups and it is possible the VAT situation could change even more. But, at the time of writing this book, selling your own ebooks online remains fraught with difficulties.

Of course, when you sell your ebooks through Amazon, Smashwords, Apple, Kobo, Barnes and Noble etc, the EU VAT is handled by these companies.

9

Formatting a Document for Kindle

Formatting a book for Kindle is quite easy, but the thing to bear in mind is that irrespective of whether you are formatting your ebook in Word or using software, the conversion process does not like tabs or indents made by using the spacebar. Indents and such like must always be done using the style menus.

Formatting Software

If you wish to take the pain out of formatting it is now possible to use software to do this for you.

1. Kindle Create is free software which you can download from kdp.amazon.com. This is user-friendly software for both Windows PC and Apple Mac computers. You can import .doc or .docx files and apply formatting to your text from within the software which will also allow you to insert images. If your Word file already has an image this will transfer over when you import the file. It will apply an automatic NCX TOC file, the one which operates from the Kindle 'GoTo' button, although if you want a TOC at the beginning of your book you will need to do that in Word before you import the file.

2. Vellum, which is also easy to use, is software designed solely for Mac users. It is not available for PCs and it is not free. It does, however, produce all the different formats for those other ebooks as well as print books from an imported Word document which must be a .docx file. The software does not accept the older Word .doc files.

Other free conversion software includes Calibre and Sigil.

Formatting a Word Document

Microsoft Word has hidden formatting which can play havoc with your file during the conversion process. So, before you follow the instructions to remove all formatting, there are certain steps to go through to ensure that Microsoft Word does not replace all the formatting you've been at pains to remove.

The instructions that follow are for Word 2016. If you are working with an early version of Word which still uses the classic menu style, rather than the newer ribbon interface, refer to Appendix One for instructions.

The primary instructions are for using Word on a PC, although I have tried to cater for Mac computer users as well.

Word for Mac is, in the main, similar to Word 2016, but where there are differences I have noted these in the instructions. Every instruction starts with the PC version and where there are differences, the instructions for Mac follow.

Preparing your Word document

You need to do this in a blank document prior to inserting your format free file into the new document, or before selecting the 'Clear Formatting' command in your current document, depending on which approach you use.

1. Open a new Word file.

2. Autocorrect options:-

    a) PC – Select the 'File' tab on the 'Ribbon' along the top of your document, and from the sidebar select 'Options'. In the 'Word Options' window, select 'Proofing' and then click the 'AutoCorrect Options' button.

    b) Mac – 'Autocorrect' is accessed by clicking 'Word' on the top menu bar and choosing 'Preferences'.

3. PC and Mac – Click on the 'AutoCorrect' Tab in the dialog box and remove the ticks from all boxes. Once you have done this the 'Auto Correct' box should have no ticks.

4. AutoFormat options:-

    a) PC – Click on the 'AutoFormat' tab at the top of the box. In the top section 'Apply' remove all ticks. In the next section 'Replace' remove all ticks except for 'Straight quotes with Smart quotes', 'Hyphens (--) with (–)', and 'Fractions'. In the bottom section 'Preserve' keep the 'Styles' box ticked.

    b) Mac – Click on the 'AutoText' tab and remove all the ticks.

5. PC and Mac – Click on the tab 'AutoFormat As You Type'. All tick boxes should be empty except for the 'Straight quotes', 'Hyphens', and 'Fractions' boxes, as above.

6. PC only – Click on the 'Actions' tab and remove all ticks.

Step 1

Removing formatting from your Word document

There are two methods of removing the formatting in your Word document. I will discuss the nuclear method first and then the alternative method which you can do from inside your original Word document.

You can remove the formatting from your file without going to the extreme of the nuclear approach. However, if you are having problems with your file after conversion, you may have to take it back to the beginning and do the nuclear option.

Always work with your formatting turned on (it looks like a backwards-facing P). You will find it in the 'Paragraph Group' in the 'Home' tab. This enables you to see paragraph returns, tabs, and any other formatting in your document.

NB. If your book is a .docx file it is safer to save it as a .doc file, an earlier version of a Word document file. Some ebook conversion processes can react unpredictably with a .docx file.

Using the nuclear approach

Please note the nuclear approach is optional. However, it ensures your document is completely devoid of any of Microsoft's sneaky hidden formatting. But you must make sure you paste the resulting document into a new Word document with all the auto formatting and auto correct options switched off, otherwise Word will replace the formatting which has been removed.

1. Open your Word file. Delete all page numbers, headers, and footers.

2. Select All:-

   a) PC – Click the 'Home' tab and in the 'Editing' group click the Select' button then click on 'Select All' from the drop down menu.

   b) Mac – Access 'Select All' in 'Edit' on the top menu bar of Word for Mac.

This will select your entire document ready for the next stage.

3. Copy document:-

   a) PC and Mac – Copy your entire document using the 'Copy' command in the 'Home' tab or by using the keyboard shortcut CTL+C.

   b) Mac – The 'Copy' command is also in the 'Edit' menu on the top menu bar of Word for Mac.

Copy your entire document then close your Word file and keep it as a backup.

4. Text Editor:-

   a) PC – Open the text editor, Windows Notepad. You'll find it in the 'All Programs; Accessories' on your computer, which you access from the Windows 'Start' button in the taskbar. Or you can type 'Notepad' into the 'Search' box. If you prefer, you can use any other text editor, as long as it is not Word.

   b) Mac – If you are using a Mac computer you can use

TextEdit which you will find in the 'Applications' folder in 'Finder'.

5. Paste your document into Notepad or the text editor of your choice using the 'Paste' command in the 'Home' tab, or by using the keyboard shortcut CTL+V. This will strip all the formatting out and you will have a plain text document.

6. Open Microsoft Word so that it is showing a new document, making sure you've turned off all the auto-formatting as described in the previous section, because if you don't, Word will put in all the hidden formatting again!

7. In your text editor, select all your text using the keyboard shortcut CTL+A, then copy it using CTL+C, and paste it into your clean Word document CTL+V. You now have your clean Word document minus all formatting.

A word of caution!

There can be a rogue tab in the document after this process, so do a search for 'Tabs' using Word's 'Find' command.

a) PC – click on the arrow beside 'Find' in the 'Editing' group on the 'Home' tab. In the drop down menu, click on 'Advanced Find', in the window that opens. Click on 'More' at the bottom, and then on 'Special'. Click on 'Tab Character' and then on 'Find Next' until you have located all of the tabs which might remain in your document.

b) Mac – To locate 'Advanced Find and Replace' in Word for Mac, click on 'Edit' in the top menu bar, then expand 'Find' in the drop down menu. Then follow the instructions above.

Now you are ready to format your document prior to the kindle conversion.

Using the alternative approach

As previously said, the nuclear approach described above is

optional and you can strip the formatting using this alternative process. However, remember to turn off all the AutoCorrect and AutoFormat options in your file first. If this approach results in errors or glitches in your converted file you may then have to consider reformatting using the nuclear approach.

Remember to work with your formatting turned on (it looks like a backwards-facing P). You will find it in the 'Paragraph Group' in the 'Home' tab. This enables you to see paragraph returns, tabs, and any other formatting in your document.

NB. As mentioned previously, if your book is a .docx file it is safer to save it as a .doc file, an earlier version of Word document files.

1. Open your Word file. Delete all page numbers, headers, and footers.

2. Select All:-

   a) PC – Click the 'Home' tab and in the 'Editing' group click the arrow at the side of the 'Select' button then click on 'Select All' from the drop down menu.

   b) Mac – Access 'Select All' in 'Edit' on the top menu bar.

This will select your entire document ready for the next stage.

3. Clear Formatting:-

   a) PC – Click the arrow at the lower right-hand side of the 'Styles' group. There are two arrows in this area. You want the one that points down and says 'More' when you hover your mouse over it. In the drop down menu, select 'Clear Formatting'.

   b) Mac – If you are using a Mac computer, the 'Clear Formatting' command is found in 'Edit' on the top menu bar, as well as in the drop down menu. This can be accessed by clicking the arrow at the side of the 'Styles' button.

This strips all the formatting from your document. You can miss this step if you are sure you do not have any fancy formatting in your document, no tabs, and no space bar spacing to make tabs etc, but I wouldn't advise it.

4. Check the document for any tabs that have not been removed. They need to be deleted.

5. Make sure any further formatting to your document remains based on 'Normal' which you can check in the 'Styles Pane'; see 'Creating Styles' below.

Step 2

Reformatting the document

After you have removed all formatting from your document you will be left with plain text with no formatting at all. If you are sure you are working with a clean file you can start to reformat the text.

All new formatting should be based on 'Normal', and you must ensure you are working from 'styles' which you access from the 'Styles' group in the 'Home' tab. Do not be tempted to format using any of the short cut icons.

The easiest way to format your document using styles is to create your own styles and give each style an individual name so you can recognize it in the 'Styles' gallery. If you use Word's auto-generated styles you run the risk of including formatting that the ebook conversion process might not like.

Creating styles

It is not too difficult to create your own styles in Word 2016.

a) PC – You do this from the 'Style Pane' which you access by clicking the small arrow at the right-hand side of the 'Styles' group. Make sure you click on the lower arrow which points to the right, not the one pointing down which is part of the group. When you hover your mouse over this arrow it will say 'Styles (Alt+Ctrl+Shift+S)'. Alternatively you could apply these keystrokes to open the 'Styles Pane', although I don't actually have enough fingers to do this.

b) Mac – Word for Mac has a 'Styles Pane' in the Word ribbon on the 'Home' tab, so it is more easily found.

Once the 'Styles' pane opens you will see a list of the styles already in use. Place your cursor on 'Normal' then click the left-hand icon at the bottom of the pane (PC) which will open the 'Create New Style From Formatting' window. (In Word for Mac, click on 'New Style' to open the 'New Style' window). Always remember to give your style a unique name so that it can easily be found in the 'Styles' group. I use names like 'Kindle Indented Para', 'Kindle First Para', 'Kindle Centred' and 'Kindle Chapter Title'.

The first window of the dialog box is for your style name and font options. After you have set these, click on 'Format' at the lower left corner for more options. The option I use most is 'Paragraph'. When you click this, the paragraph box opens and you can set your spacing, indentation, and alignment here. After you have entered your choices, click 'OK' to return to the main window.

a) PC – Now, put ticks in the boxes next to 'Add to Styles Gallery', 'Automatically Update', and 'New Document based on this Template'.

b) Mac – In Word for Mac the choices are slightly different. Add ticks next to 'Add to template', 'Add to Quick Style list' and 'Automatically update'.

Click 'OK' to exit the dialog box, and if you check the 'Styles' group you will find your new style there.

Formatting instructions

The instructions are for an indented prose style.

1. Select All:-

a) PC – Click the 'Home' tab and in the 'Editing' group click the arrow at the side of the 'Select' button then click on 'Select All' from the drop down menu.

b) Mac – Access 'Select All' in 'Edit' on the top menu bar.

This will select your entire document ready for the next stage.

2. Creating a style (refer to the above instruction):-

   a) PC – Open the 'Create New Style From Formatting' window. Insert a title, for example, 'Kindle indented', choose a font, and then open the 'Paragraph' dialog box after clicking on 'Format'.

   b) Mac – Open the 'New Style' window in Word for Mac and follow the same instructions for the PC.

3. Select the following in the paragraph box:-

   i) Alignment: 'Left'.

   ii) Special: 'First Line' – 'By' '0.5' – (Smashwords prefers 0.3 in this box. So do I). These sizes are in inches. If your measurements are metric, simply convert them to the metric equivalent.

   iii) Line Spacing: 'Single'. It is important to make sure that there is absolutely nothing in the 'At' box, as apparently, this can really mess up your document. Note, for prose there is nothing in the 'Spacing' boxes 'Before' and 'After' nor the 'Indentation' boxes. Click 'OK'.

   iv) If you haven't already done this, remember to tick the style options in the main window ('Add to Styles Gallery', 'Automatically update', and 'New documents based on this template'), and to replace 'Style 1' with an easily identifiable name of your choice. For example, 'Kindle Indented'.

   v) Click 'OK'.

This will give you an appropriately formatted prose document. Note, however, that the headings are no longer how they should be, therefore these will also have to be formatted.

4. Alternatively, if you wish a block paragraph style such as might be more suited to poetry or nonfiction, create a block

paragraph style following the above instructions but in the 'Paragraph' box format your paragraphs like this. Change the 'Spacing' section to '6pt After'. This gives you a space between paragraphs. Change 'Special' to 'None'. Click 'OK'.

Back to formatting the prose style now. You will see that the title etc is now sitting in the wrong place, so what we have to do is go back and centre it all, plus put in a page break.

5. Highlight your title and anything else on the title page. Refer to the above instruction on creating a style and open the 'Create New Style From Formatting' window (or 'the 'New Style' window in Word for Mac). Insert a title, for example, 'Kindle Centred', choose a font, and then open the 'Paragraph' dialog box after clicking on 'Format'.

6. Change 'Alignment' to 'Centered'. Change 'Special' to 'None'. Do not forget the 'Special' box otherwise your title will be off centre. Click 'OK'.

7. Before you exit the new style window don't forget to tick the style options as previously described.

Now you need to separate your title from the beginning of your book so you need to put in a line break.

8. Place your cursor on the last return on your title page and then click on the 'Insert' tab. In the 'Pages' group click the 'Page Break' command button. In Word for Mac you can also find the 'Page Break' command in the 'Insert' menu on the top menu bar.

9. Now go through your document and centre headings, chapters or titles in the same way you did your title page. If you have asterisks between scenes, centre them too. Provided you have created a style, perhaps named 'Kindle Centred' you simply highlight the section and click the style.

If you want your chapters to start on a new page follow the same instructions for placing a page break as was indicated for the title page. This is for Kindle only. Do not put page breaks between chapters for Smashwords. The meatgrinder (autovetter) does it automatically, provided the word 'Chapter' is in the heading. If you put page breaks in as well it may result in blank pages between chapters.

If you want a page at the end of your book for an author bio, insert a page break at the end and then add the details you want. If you add other published books and intend to use Smashwords as well as Kindle, they consider themselves the publisher and don't like references to other publishers. If you add other publisher details or hyperlinks to other publishers, apart from Smashwords, your book won't be accepted for the Premium collection and therefore won't be distributed to the Apple iBooks store, Barnes and Noble etc. You can, however, refer to your books as being available at all major bookstores as long as names are not mentioned.

If you want extra spaces anywhere in the manuscript do not use paragraph returns to do this. *Smashwords Style Guide* says no more than two paragraph returns should be used to avoid blank pages but in reality, I have found that even one paragraph return can result in a blank page. If you want additional space use the 'Before' and 'After' spacing fields in the paragraph box, but ensure the maximum space used is no more than 10pts.

The only place you should ever use additional paragraph returns is your Title or Copyright page and your additional information page at the end of the book.

And never, ever indent using the space bar or tabs! Do everything through the Paragraph Styling Box.

Adding Metadata

Before you leave your formatted document you need to add the metadata. If you do not add this, the book's metadata will say 'untitled' when the top of the eReader screen is clicked.

With your document open:-

a) PC instructions:-

    i) Click the 'File' tab;

ii) Click 'Info' in the sidebar;

iii) Under 'Properties' at the right-hand side of the page, check that your name is there as the author. If it isn't, click 'Add an Author' and enter it;

iv) Click on 'Add a Title' and enter the title of your book;

v) Click on 'Add a Tag' and enter tags that relate to the content of your book, eg the tag I have added for this book is 'guide to self-publishing';

vi) Click 'Add a Category' and enter a category to describe what kind of book it is, eg fiction, nonfiction, crime fiction, or whatever is appropriate;

vii) Return to document.

b) Mac instructions:-

i) Click 'File' in the top menu;

ii) Click 'Properties' in the drop down menu;

iii) Click the 'Summary' tab and add the title of your book, author name, and keywords to describe searchable content for the book;

iv) Click 'OK'.

You should now save your document.

Hints and tips

Indentation: One conversion problem I have noticed that occurs during the process of making a Kindle version of your book is that paragraphs which are not indented have an indent after conversion.

In works of fiction, the first paragraph does not usually have an indent, although all other paragraphs do. If you don't mind your first paragraph being indented then you do not need to do anything. However, if you prefer the non-indented paragraph to remain, there is a workaround and it is quite simple.

Your indented paragraphs will be either 0.3 or 0.5 of an inch or the metric equivalent, so the answer is to apply an indent to the first paragraph as well. This indent should be as small as you can make it so that it is hardly visible, but is recognized as an indent by the conversion process. I usually apply an indent of 0.05 of an inch which is 0.127cms.

Heading styles: Never use the Word auto-generated heading styles, they have hidden formatting. Make your own heading styles.

Formatting for Kindle checklist

Did you remember:-

1. To turn on your formatting so you can see if there is any rogue formatting remaining – in particular, any tabs and any additional paragraph returns. If any are found, delete them;

2. To get rid of headers, footers and page numbering;

3. To clear all formatting prior to reformatting;

4. To check that all new formatting is based on 'Normal';

5. To centre your title page and copyright page;

6. To centre all chapter headings and any other headings you have;

7. To centre scene dividers or asterisks (if you have them);

8. To put in page breaks between chapters for Kindle only – not Smashwords;

9. To add metadata;

10. To check that the only paragraph returns in your document are those required to start a new paragraph. There should be no other paragraph returns anywhere else in your manuscript with the exception of Title, copyright and back pages;

11. To check the ebook in Kindle Previewer before publishing.

10

Preparing Your Ebook for Upload

You now have your formatted Word document ready for upload to your preferred ebook seller, and of course, the leader in the field is the mighty Amazon with its Kindle eReader. So we will concentrate on the KDP upload process.

But, before we do that, there is one final hurdle to cross, and that is the provision of a TOC (Table of Contents) with live links.

When ebooks first started to be published there was no necessity for a TOC, and some of my earlier books do not possess one.

Things have moved on over the years and most ebook distributors now require a TOC. I must say I have mixed feelings about this. A TOC is a valuable asset to a nonfiction book because it provides a road map to the contents of the book, and you can pick and choose which part of the book you wish to read. However, I am sure I am not alone in finding several pages of a TOC in a fiction book which simply reads; Chapter 1, Chapter 2, Chapter 3 ad infinitum, to be excessive. My latest novel has seventy chapters and I certainly do not want to read a TOC that length, nor can I justify why it would be needed.

I have got around that problem by making an abbreviated version of a TOC. I usually insert live links at the beginning of the book, such as; Dedication, Acknowledgements, Beginning (which starts at Chapter 1), About the Author, and Other Books. This satisfies the requirement of a TOC with live links without boring the reader with a list of numbered chapters.

The instructions for the addition of a TOC will work on the assumption that it will be the abbreviated version. However, if you are using chapter headings simply add the headings you wish. The procedure is the same irrespective of the headings you choose.

Adding a TOC

A word of warning before you start – it is not a good idea to use Word's auto-TOC generating feature because it works with the heading styles therefore there is a risk the TOC may not convert properly. A safer way to generate your TOC is contained in the step-by-step instructions that follow.

Start by typing your table of contents at the beginning of the book, preferably after the copyright page. Use a normal paragraph style, or an appropriate style you have created. Do not use one of Word's heading styles.

But before you can link the contents you need to bookmark the pages in your manuscript that correspond with the items in the table.

Working with the headings in your book

1. Highlight the heading in your book where you want to create the link. For example, 'Dedication'. Only highlight the words you need with no extras.

2. Setting bookmarks:-

   a) PC – Click the 'Insert' tab and in the 'Links' group click the 'Bookmark' button. In the dialog box which opens, type your heading at the top eg 'Dedication' (type one word – no spaces – and it must start with a letter) and then click 'Add'. This places the bookmark in the list underneath.

   b) Mac – In Word for Mac you can access the 'Bookmark' dialog box in two ways. You can access it as described above, or through the 'Insert' menu on the top menu bar. Once you have accessed it, follow the instructions for a PC.

3. Repeat with every heading you wish to include in your TOC. It is important to use only one word with no spaces in the dialog box, for example, if you choose to do Chapter One, name that as c1, ch1, or chap1 or something similar, or just remove the space in the middle.

If I wanted to bookmark this section, I would simply name it 'TOC' in the 'Bookmark' dialog box. This would easily be identifiable when it comes to linking my bookmark with the full heading of 'Adding a TOC' in my table of contents.

Working with your Table of Contents

1. Go to your table of contents at the front of the book.

2. Highlight the first entry in the table, eg 'Dedication'. It is important to link all of the text in the entry. For example, to create a link to my bookmark 'TOC' which marks a place in the document 'Adding a TOC (Table of Contents)' would have to be highlighted in the table on the 'Contents' page.

3. Click the 'Insert' tab and in the 'Links' group click the 'Hyperlink' button (In Word for Mac you can also access the 'Hyperlink' command in the 'Insert' menu on the top menu bar). In the dialog box which opens, choose 'Place in This Document' which is in the left-hand column (or select the tab, 'This Document', in Word for Mac). In the table displayed, under 'Bookmarks', select the heading that matches the one in your TOC, and then click 'OK'. (If you are working on a Mac computer you will need to click on the arrow beside 'Bookmarks' in order to see the bookmarks you have created.) You now have a live link from your TOC to the relevant place in your book.

4. Continue to link your table of contents in this fashion until every link is made.

5. Test every link by clicking in the TOC and checking that every link leads to the correct page.

Creating an account in KDP (Kindle Direct Publishing)

1. Sign up to KDP at KDP.Amazon.com using your Amazon.com username and password to sign in. If you do not have an Amazon.com account you will need to create one. You can do this from the KDP homepage by clicking 'Sign Up'. Provide the details asked for and then select 'I am a new customer'. If you are uncertain whether your current Amazon account includes Amazon.com try signing in first and if this fails, create the new account.

2. Agree to the Kindle Direct Publishing Terms of Service.

3. The Dashboard opens with headings 'Bookshelf'; 'Reports'; 'Community'; and 'KDP Select'. In the top right-hand corner of the page, it will say 'Your account information is incomplete'. Click the 'Update Now' button.

4. Company/Publisher Information: Enter the following:-

   i) The name you use for tax purposes, that can either be your own name or the name of your company;

   ii) Your country of residence;

   iii) Your address, postcode and phone number.

5. Tax Information: This is your tax status under US law and the information required is provided by you in the tax interview. In this section click the 'Complete Tax Information' button and provide all the information requested. It is no longer necessary for you to have a US tax number for your US sales. Your UK National Insurance Number is now acceptable. However, if you do have a US tax number, either an ITIN or EIN, the latter is no longer accepted for the tax interview due to a change in US tax legislation.

6. Payment Information: Choose how you want to be paid. If

you wish KDP to pay directly into your bank account, which is the easiest way, you will have to add your bank details. If you do not add them KDP will pay you by cheque and you may find that banks charge a fee for cashing this.

7. Finally, click 'Save', and your account information is complete.

Uploading books

1. Sign into your KDP dashboard and go to your Bookshelf.

2. Click 'Add New Title' or 'Create New Title', or click the square underneath which says 'Kindle eBook'. Amazon has been making some changes recently, so it could be any of those. This will take you to Kindle eBook Details, the first page of the publishing process.

3. Kindle eBook Details: Enter the following:-

   i) Language;

   ii) Title;

   iii) Subtitle;

   iv) Series Information;

   v) Edition Number (unless your book has been previously published and this edition is different from the original, this will be 1, or you could leave it blank);

   vi) Author;

   vii) Contributor (best to leave this blank unless you have a co-author because there is a risk that the contributor will be listed as a co-author);

   viii) Description (the description you want to appear on Amazon's selling page);

   ix) Publishing Rights (where you indicate whether you own the copyright);

   x) Keywords (this affects search results so think carefully);

xi) Categories (you choose from a list);

xii) Age and Grade Range (optional and applies to children's books).

4. Click 'Save and Continue'.

5. Kindle eBook Content:-

i) Manuscript: Browse your computer for the file to upload;

ii) Click yes or no to enable DRM (Digital Rights Management) this is easily cracked so I've never seen the point of putting it on, plus it annoys readers if they want to read the ebook on different devices;

iii) Upload Cover: JPEG or Tiff formats only;

iv) Kindle eBook Preview: You have a choice of using the online previewer, downloading a copy to your computer to view on Kindle Previewer, or downloading to your Kindle. I usually choose computer because that also gives you a file you can send out to reviewers;

v) Kindle eBook ISBN: You do not need an ISBN for a Kindle ebook because Amazon lists it as an ASIN and they do not provide statistics to the ISBN agencies on the numbers of ebooks sold.

There is also a space in this box for Publisher, either leave this blank or fill in your own name or the name of your imprint. You do not need to be a publishing company to apply an imprint name to your book.

6. Click 'Save and Continue'.

7. Kindle eBook Pricing:-

i) KDP Select Enrolment: Only select this if you wish your book to be exclusive to Amazon;

ii) Territories: Select all the territories where you hold the distribution rights eg 'All Territories' if no one else has publishing rights, or select the specific territories where you hold the rights;

iii) Royalty and Pricing: Select the royalty rate, 70% for

books priced between £1.99/$2.99 and £9.99/$9.99, or 35% if they are priced lower than the minimum price or higher than the maximum price. You can base all the other markets on the Amazon dollar price or you can set your own price for the UK and other markets;

iv) Matchbook: This is optional. It allows you to sell your book at a reduced price or give it for free to customers who have bought the paperback;

v) Book Lending: This option is already ticked and locked if you have chosen the 70% royalty rate. This allows customers who have bought your ebook to lend it to their friends and family for 14 days;

vi) Terms and Conditions: The tick box for this seems to have vanished in preference for the assumption if you choose 'Publish' you have agreed to them. However, if there is a tick box to agree to this, make sure it is ticked.

8. Click 'Publish Your Kindle eBook', alternatively, you can save it as a draft.

Other self-publishing companies

Now that you have published your ebook to KDP you may want to turn your mind to the other options for self-publishing ebooks, namely Smashwords and Draft2Digital. The procedure should be very similar, and Mark Coker's guide to publishing to Smashwords is invaluable.

One thing to remember when uploading to Smashwords is to delete any page breaks between chapters because the formatting process automatically inserts a page break provided the word Chapter is in the heading.

The other thing to note is that if you have published with KDP you should opt out of the Amazon distribution channel in the Smashwords Channel Manager and likewise with any other distributor you intend to use to publish ebooks.

11

Pricing an Ebook

In the early days of the internet, it was a bit of a free for all. There was an expectation that everything found online should be free. This led to the rise of pirate websites where anyone could obtain an illegal version of anything, such as, music, films, videos, computer software, and anything else that could be downloaded. When eReaders came onto the market, ebooks written by best-selling authors were also added to these sites. The problem was that the people who downloaded pirate copies of whatever they wanted did not see it as illegal.

This situation continued until the music industry got tough and leaned on the internet service providers to make them apply sanctions to those subscribers using pirate websites to obtain illegal downloads. So, if you are a user of PirateBay or any other pirate websites, and download illegal copies of anything do not be surprised if your broadband provider pulls the plug and cuts off your access to the internet. In the meantime, before the plug was pulled, you may also have populated your computer with malware and viruses.

However, irrespective of whether the pirate websites existed, there was an expectation that all printed matter, such as newspapers, magazines, and ebooks, should be free. This expectation is still alive in a number of internet users who will never spend money on an ebook, preferring to download all the free copies that are available. This is the reason that the offer of a free ebook may result in thousands of downloads but does not necessarily improve the sales of an author's other books. In some cases it can also lead to negative reviews due to indiscriminate downloading of a genre the reader does not enjoy.

When you are pricing your ebook you might want to bear in mind that there would appear to be a distinct division between ebook buyers. There is the group who will only buy cheap ebooks, either free or in the 99 pence range. Then there are the readers who buy books because they like the author, or the story appeals to them. These are the readers who will buy your ebook without taking the price into consideration, although I would advise you not to exceed £5.99 which is the top end for a self-published book, although traditionally published ebooks are often higher than this. But, better still, keep the price somewhere between the £2.99 to £4.99 range. I have found that the sweet spot for my ebooks is £3.99.

12

Cost of Publishing an Ebook

This will vary in accordance with how much of the work you do yourself and how much you outsource. If you do everything, from editing, formatting, and cover design, you will have no costs at all, because publication through KDP is free.

However, if you want your book to look professional and be the best book you can provide for your readers, you would be well advised to invest in editing and a book cover as the very minimum. If it is a choice between the two, choose the book cover, and try to find some beta readers to advise on the story. A beta reader can never replace a professional editor but some of them are very good and many authors have a pool of beta readers who will read their books prior to publication.

Editing costs are variable. Some editors charge according to how many words or pages are in the book. Others charge by the amount of time they take to edit the book. Some of them will ask to see several chapters before providing an estimate so they can assess how much time they are liable to spend on the editing task. An approximation is that it takes one hour to edit ten pages, although this estimation will depend on how much editing is required on each page.

It is in your own interests to do as much editing and polishing as you possibly can before approaching an editor. The cleaner and more polished a manuscript you produce will result in less editing time being needed.

Finding an editor

1. SfEP (Society for Editors and Proofreaders) have a directory of editors at sfep.org.uk.

2. Reedsy is another place with a list of professional editors at reedsy.com.

3. If you subscribe to become a member of ALLi (Alliance of Independent Authors) you will find many editors among their members.

Approximate costs

1. Editing: SfEP (Society for Editors and Proofreaders) recommends a minimum hourly rate of £22.75 per hour for proofreading, and £26.50 per hour for copy-editing, however, the cost of editing is something that is negotiable between author and editor. SfEP indicates it takes, on average, one hour to edit ten pages.

2. Book Cover: A Google search of book cover designers should result in a wide choice of designers at varying prices, including those who offer starving author rates, initially cheap with the expectation of higher charges once an author has become successful.

I would estimate that you could commission a book cover within the price range of £100 up to £1,000 or higher. However, there are book covers and book covers! So, I would suggest you look at a designer's previous covers and choose one who designs covers that will suit the kind of book you have written.

3. Formatting: If you can master the skill of formatting your own ebook this is certainly the cheapest option. It is not too difficult to format your own ebook, although it can be tricky the first time you do it. For those who are unable to master the process, there are individuals and firms which specialize in formatting. Once again a Google search on ebook formatting should provide a selection. The price range is between £100 to £500 depending on what you want.

13

Publishing a Paperback

I am assuming the book you have written has by now been edited to the nth degree. You have expunged all the typos, cleaned up the grammar, ensured there are no plot holes and the story flows well. You've made it the best book it could possibly be and you are ready to launch it into the world as a paperback.

But wait a minute! Before you consider uploading or sending your files to your chosen publisher or printer, there are some other things you need to have ready.

There is nothing worse than being faced with an upload page demanding information you haven't prepared. It might be a demand for the description of your book in 25 words, or 300 words, or 500 words, or worse still 500 characters, and you haven't a clue how many words or characters are in your description. You do have one, don't you? If you don't you could be in the situation of having to stop in the middle of the process to write the description, and believe me, it won't be your best effort if it is done in a hurry. Far better to have everything prepared beforehand.

Make a list of what you think you might need prior to submitting your files for publication.

1. The text of your book (naturally).

2. The book cover: If you employ a cover designer they will supply the cover as a PDF, otherwise, you will have the hassle of preparing this yourself.

3. Blurbs or descriptions of your book, both short and long, and

make sure you know the number of characters as well as words so you will know it fits, otherwise part of your description might be lopped off and you don't want that. And don't forget that the space between words counts as a character.

4. ISBN if you've bought your own.

5. Price: I hope you've taken into consideration shipping or postal charges plus store discounts before deciding this.

6. Genre and tags: What kind of book is it? Decide this beforehand so that you have the appropriate tags ready.

Now, take a deep breath and start the publication process with your chosen publisher or printer.

Self-publishing services

The most popular companies providing self-publishing services are KDP (Kindle Direct Publishing) and IngramSpark. Other self-publishing companies, including Lulu.com, FeedaRead, Matador and several more, can supply packages of services. Then there are the aggregators who will provide distribution if you publish with them. Smashwords or Draft2Digital lead the pack in this field of self-publishing. If you simply want a book printing service, Clays, and also Book Printing UK provide a reasonably priced service, and of course, you can contact local printing firms to request estimates. Always ask to see copies of any company's previously printed books before you place your order.

Basic questions to ask when engaging any self-publishing service, whether this is for basic printing or a full package of services include the following. What is the service being offered? What does it include? How do I get it? What does it cost? Will there be any extras? Are they a bona fide company or are they on any writer beware lists? Where can I obtain references? And, most importantly, are they upfront about the costs involved?

A useful guide, compiled by the Watchdog team at the Alliance of Independent Authors (ALLi) is free to ALLi members but is also available to buy online. *How to Choose A Self-Publishing Service 2016: A Writer's Guide from the Alliance of Independent Authors* (updated every year) is a mine of information. It lists many of the companies providing author services, indicating costs and what you can expect for the money. It details which companies provide the best services as well as those to be wary of. In my view, this guide is essential reading for the author considering buying services rather than taking the do-it-yourself approach.

Author services and outsourcing

Some authors will prefer to do everything themselves and if this is the case there is no, or very little cost. Others, however, lack the time, experience, or confidence to take this approach and for them, it is a matter of buying author services from a company or outsourcing the specific tasks they require.

The two most important tasks it is advisable to outsource are editing and cover creation.

Outsourcing is probably more time consuming than buying a package of author services from a reputable self-publishing company. If you outsource the services you will have to search for, check out, and negotiate terms with a variety of professionals providing these services.

Engaging a self-publishing company which specializes in offering author services means you can buy a complete package which usually includes cover creation, formatting, and in many cases editing, as well as distribution and marketing.

Reputable companies will allow you to pick and mix, contracting for some of their services and not others.

While it is perfectly acceptable to pay for the services you require, one thing you should not have to pay for is the actual publication of the book, although there may well be a small setup fee, for example, IngramSpark charges a $49 setup fee for each book they publish for you.

If there is a fee of several thousand pounds for publishing costs, over and above the cost of the author services provided, it is likely that you are dealing with one of the less reputable self-publishing companies and are dipping your toes into the vanity publishing trade where the only customer they are interested in selling to, is you.

Finding the services you require, whether you wish to outsource certain parts of the task or buy a full self-publishing package can be fraught with difficulties when you try to separate genuine services from the sharks in the self-publishing business.

Guidelines and tips on what to look out for are contained in the article *General Guidelines and Tips on Avoiding Scams* posted by the Critters Workshop at critters.org. This article has a lot of good advice and is well worth reading.

Preditors and Editors at pred-ed.com was always a good website to guide the unwary. However, it currently seems to be inactive, although it is worth keeping an eye out for them to reappear online.

The SFWA (Science Fiction and Fantasy Writers of America) Writer Beware website at www.sfwa.org is a good place to check out companies and they have lists of vanity publishers as well as advice on what to watch out for.

There are also various forums on the internet where you can request information from members on the validity or otherwise of a company you may be considering. One of these is the Absolute Write forum at absolutewrite.com but there are many others.

As well as checking the internet for information about self-publishing services and companies, a small investment in the book, previously mentioned, *How to Choose a Self-Publishing Service 2016: A Writer's Guide from The Alliance of Independent Authors*, is money well spent. You can find this book at all the good ebook stores but, of course, if you subscribe to ALLi (Alliance of Independent Authors) you can download a free copy from their website. Subscription to ALLi also gives you access to their closed Facebook page which is a mine of useful information and a place where any question you might have, can be answered. The other advantage of a subscription is access to a variety of services at discounted prices.

14

The ISBN and Distribution

ISBN

All books distributed by traditional publishers have an ISBN on the back cover and in the front matter of their books.

Likewise, the self-publisher will need an ISBN and they have two options: the free one supplied by the printers or publishers of their print book, or the option of purchasing their own ISBNs from Neilsen in the UK, Bowker in the US, or from the ISBN agency in the self-publishers country of residence. ISBNs are international and can only be bought in the author or publisher's country of residence irrespective of where they intend to market and sell their books. These agencies can easily be found with a simple internet search for ISBN agency and naming the country.

The person who owns the ISBN, whether that be yourself or the company you choose to print your books, will be registered as the publisher.

ISBN stands for International Standard Book Number, and the only use they have is for identification. If there is no need for identification eg if you publish a short run of your memoir for personal distribution, you don't actually need one and there is no legal imperative for you to have one. Identification is needed for the purposes of ordering, distribution, fulfilment, and payment. It identifies you as the publisher of the book for selling purposes, and it allows the distributor and shop to know where payment should be sent.

In the norm, print books should have an ISBN, and you can

either buy the ISBN yourself from Nielsen or take advantage of the free one KDP can supply.

A word of warning here. The free ISBN from KDP makes them your publisher, you cannot then have the book printed anywhere else, and bookstores and distributors in the UK will not order from KDP because it is an Amazon company.

If you buy your own ISBN, it makes you the publisher. Orders from bookstores and distributors will come directly to you, and you will be responsible for filling these orders.

The other advantage is that you can have your books printed by KDP for the Amazon market, and you can have them printed by your own printer in the UK for the UK market. The downside is it costs £159 for a block of 10, or £89 for a single ISBN.

ISBNs can be bought from Neilsen at nielsenbook.co.uk if you are based in the UK, Ireland, or a British Overseas Territory, and Bowker in the US. If you are based elsewhere you can find your national ISBN Agency on the International ISBN Agency's website.

When you are assessing how many ISBNs you might need, it is important to remember that if you intend to publish your book in different formats, such as, paperback, ebook, hardback, or even a different size of paperback from the original, or a new edition, you will need a different ISBN for each version and each format. The ISBN you use on your book is not interchangeable.

Nielsen has recently established the Nielsen ISBN Store. Prior to setting up this store, ISBNs could only be bought in blocks of ten, but there is now an option to buy an individual ISBN if this is all you think you will ever require.

However, the cost of an individual ISBN is exorbitant when compared to the cost of blocks, with the cost of an individual ISBN decreasing in relation to the amount bought.

The prices, at the time of writing, are £89.00 for a single ISBN; £159.00 (£15.90 each) per block of ten; £359.00 (£3.59 each) per block of one hundred; and £949.00 (95 pence each) per block of one thousand. As you can see, even if you only require two, then you are cheaper with a block of ten. In addition to the cost of the ISBNs, you will be charged a registration fee for a first time purchase. This fee is not charged for subsequent purchases.

Kindle published ebooks do not require an ISBN because Amazon has its own identifier, the ASIN. This is the way they track and identify sales. Of course, you can put an ISBN on if you want to, but this is an avoidable expense.

Other ebook publishers such as Apple iBooks, Barnes and Noble, and Kobo, do require ISBNs. Distributors such as Smashwords also need an ISBN because they need to track which seller your book has gone to, how many they have sold, and to ensure the payment is made to the correct author.

In this instance, I would recommend taking the free Smashwords ISBN, unless you plan to supply ebook retailers individually which increases your workload as a self-publisher and, in my opinion, would be a bit daft because Smashwords supplies them for you.

Adding the ISBN to your book

Assuming you have bought a block of ISBN numbers these will be registered to you as the publisher of your book or books.

You will be given a list of the numbers exclusive to your publications, probably on a spreadsheet file. Save the file to your computer in a place you will easily find it because you will need to access the file each time you publish a book. I would also advise printing the list in case anything goes wrong with your computer.

You must use a new ISBN for each book you publish, you cannot use the same ISBN for different books, so it is also a good idea to have a system where you can check which numbers are already in use.

When you make your application to Nielsen (UK) for ISBNs

you are required to provide all the details for your first ISBN use, that is, the first book you intend to self-publish using an ISBN. Nielsen will then retain a record of the book and its ISBN and this information will be available to libraries, distributors, and retailers.

Any subsequent book you publish should also be registered with Nielsen using one of your own unique ISBN numbers. You do this through Nielsen Title Editor at nielsenbook.co.uk where you can add books or edit the details of books already registered.

When adding a book you will be required to insert the ISBN you intend to use for it, before you click 'Easy Add Book' or 'Detailed Add Book'. There is also a tab you click to add your cover picture. The specifications are JPEG 24 bit, RGB Colour, or PNG 24 bit, RGB Colour. The minimum image size is 648 pixels tall. The file name for your image should be the ISBN number, and the image should be your front cover, not the full spread of front and back.

Distribution

Distribution is one area where traditional publishers have the edge. They supply wholesalers on a sale or return basis, they feature your book in their catalogues, and they may even have travelling salesmen who visit bookstores with the sole aim of selling their books. You notice I said, their books, not your books. They are in the business to make money, after all.

One of the things that new authors expect from a publishing deal is promotion and marketing, but this is unlikely for a new and unknown author. Publishing firms have restricted marketing budgets and whatever money is available is usually allocated to the bigger name authors. The new author will be expected to promote their own books in the same way that the self-publishing author does.

Smaller publishers may actually promote you a bit better than the big publishers, but they may have no better access to distribution sources than you would have if you self-published.

The two largest wholesalers in the UK are Bertrams and Gardners, but they are unlikely to keep your self-published book in stock. However, provided you use your own ISBN for your self-published book, you will get orders from both these wholesalers. These orders are usually for individual books on special order from bookstores, or a library order.

The wholesaler will expect a discounted price but you can negotiate this with them on the basis you are a small publisher. I have found them very approachable and instead of providing books at the normal 50 or 60% discount you can negotiate a lower discount rate.

It is important when working out the selling price of your book that you include the discount you will be expected to provide, plus the cost of postage, currently £2.09 or £2.85 per book depending on whether it can be posted at letter or parcel rate, otherwise you will be running at a loss.

One last thing to mention is the sale or return model the big publishers operate. Sale or return allows booksellers and distributors to return unsold books to the publisher who is expected to bear the cost of these returns. Alternatively, authority can be given to pulp (destroy) the books as a less costly option. A self-publisher cannot afford to provide books in this way so it is advisable to have a statement on your invoices indicating no sale or return. I always include this statement on my invoices – 'All sales final. No sale or return policy'.

15

Publishing a KDP Print Book

KDP (Kindle Direct Publishing)

The two main POD (Print on Demand) companies are Kindle Direct Publishing at kdp.amazon.com, and IngramSpark at ingramspark.com.

Initially, I chose to use Createspace but their print on demand service has now transferred to KDP. The information that follows refers to this company.

If you do all the design and formatting yourself publishing with KDP is free. Other POD printers may require a setup fee, although this should not be extortionate. If it is extortionate, there is a possibility it is a vanity press, and these presses should be avoided at all costs.

The KDP recommendation is to use a PDF file to upload your manuscript. However, KDP will accept a variety of file formats, such as, DOC(.doc), DOCX (.docx), HTML (.html), or RTF (.rtf). If you choose to upload your manuscript as a PDF file you must ensure that all fonts are embedded. If you find that problematic you may find it easier to do all designing, formatting, and uploading with a Microsoft Word document which KDP will then format as a PDF for publication.

The best place to investigate the publishing options for KDP is their help pages on kdp.amazon.com. You will find masses of information including the options in connection with book covers, interior design, printing options, and distribution.

KDP supplies templates for the layout of your book. You will find them in the help pages of kdp.amazon.com. There is a choice of template, either blank or formatted with sample content. The formatted template comes ready with the front matter in place, the blank one does not. These templates are the same ones previously available from Createspace.

It is important to note that all the formatting in the formatted template is contained in the page breaks, therefore it is important not to delete these when you copy your text into it. You will probably have to put in additional chapters with page breaks between. Do not do this from the last chapter in the template, do it from one of the middle ones, otherwise, you will upset your page numbers and headers. Your manuscript should be pasted in, one chapter at a time. Do not be tempted to paste the whole novel in at one go.

Remember to include metadata information in your formatted document. Full instructions on how to do this are included in chapter nine which deals with formatting for Kindle.

KDP also provides a tool for those who wish to design their own cover. Their free online Cover Creator allows you to use your own photos, images, logos and text, they even have a free image gallery with thousands of photos you can use along with the Cover Creator template to design your own cover.

Uploading a paperback to Kindle Direct Publishing

What you will need is a PDF or Word file of your novel, as well as a PDF cover, and the ISBN for your book. You will also need to decide a size for your book and the paper colour. It is important to note here that the default size is 6 x 9 inches. However, this is a US size, and UK books are different.

The most common sizes in the UK are 5 x 8 inches, or 5.5 x 8.5 inches. I chose the latter because that was the size of my traditionally published book and I wanted all my books to be a uniform size. And the paper colour for fiction in the UK is cream, although nonfiction books usually have white paper.

If you are in doubt check the sizes of books in your bookcase, making sure they are books which have recently been published because some older books used smaller sizes. And remember, the smaller the size, the more pages your book will have, and costs are based on the number of pages.

The Interior Reviewer is a useful tool to examine your uploaded file. The Reviewer displays your file online in a virtual version of your printed book and will also highlight any printing issues that have been detected during the automated print check during upload.

Using the Online Reviewer you can check every page of your manuscript to ensure everything is in order – that your text area is within the printing guides, your numbering and headers are in the correct places, and most importantly, that the text and the numbering in your book start on a right-hand page. If anything is amiss it is easy to pick it up at this stage, correct it and resubmit a new file.

Let's get started

1. Open an account with Kindle Direct Publishing at https://kdp.amazon.com. You will find information on how to do this in chapter ten, 'Preparing your Ebook for Upload'.

2. Log in to Kindle Direct Publishing.

3. On the Bookshelf screen under 'Create a New Title' click '+ Paperback'.

Paperback Details screen

Ensure the information on this page is correct before saving as some items on this page will be locked after your book has been published. The fields on this page are:-

1. Language: Self-explanatory, as I am publishing the book in the English language I put English here;

2. Book Title: This is where you enter the title of your book. If you have a subtitle, enter it in the box below, otherwise leave it blank;

3. Series Title: If your book is part of a series put the name and number of the series here;

4. Edition Number: Leave this blank unless there has been a previous edition of the book;

5. Primary Author: That's you, enter your author name;

6. Contributors: Leave this blank unless you have a co-author. Any name you put in this field will appear beside your author name on Amazon;

7. Description: Enter the description you want to appear on Amazon's selling page and it might be worthwhile spending some time on this to ensure the description makes the book look attractive to customers;

8. Publishing Rights: This is where you indicate you own the copyright to the book as well as the publishing rights. The other option is a book in the public domain but this is unlikely to apply to you unless you are publishing a book with an expired copyright, eg republishing a classic;

9. Keywords: Words that describe your book. They can be single words or word phrases separated by commas. Think carefully because keywords affect search results;

10 Categories: These are BISAC categories and you choose · from a list. BISAC means Book Industry Standards and Communications and these categories are used by the book selling industry to group and identify books by their subject matter;

11. Adult Content: Self explanatory. You tick 'No' or 'Yes'.

Click 'Save and Continue'.

The Paperback Content screen

1. Print ISBN: An ISBN is required to publish your book, and

KDP offers two options for you to choose from.

> i) Get a free KDP ISBN;
>
> ii) Use your own ISBN.

Tick the option you prefer but take into consideration previous discussions about the advisability of buying and using your own ISBN before you do so, because once the choice is made it cannot be undone.

If you intend to choose option two, using your own ISBN you must remember to ensure the book is added to the Nielsen (UK) database.

> iii) Imprint: If you have a publishing imprint this is where you insert its name. For example, my author name is Chris Longmuir, but my publishing imprint is Barker & Jansen.

2. Publication Date: If you know your publication date, enter it here, otherwise you can leave this blank.

3. Print Options:-

> i) Interior & paper type: For the interior you have a choice of 'black & white' or 'color' (KDP spelling). This refers to the text so unless you are publishing a book with colour images, tick either 'Black & white interior with cream paper' or 'Black & white interior with white paper'. Cream paper is common in the UK for fiction and white paper for nonfiction;
>
> ii) Trim Size: The default is the US size of 6 x 9. If you are publishing your book in the UK it is better to click the 'Select a different size' box and select a size more appropriate for a UK published book;
>
> iii) Bleed settings: You have two choices, 'No Bleed' or 'Bleed'. Choose 'No bleed' unless you have illustrations which need to stretch beyond the print area to each edge. If you do require 'Bleed' this option is only available if you upload a PDF file;
>
> iv) Paperback cover finish: Choose either 'Matte' or

'Glossy' for your cover finish. I have used both and I have to admit I prefer the matte finish.

4. Manuscript: Use the 'Upload paperback manuscript' button to upload your file. If your file is a PDF ensure your fonts are embedded (information on embedding fonts is contained in Chapter 16), alternatively you can upload a Word, HTML, or RTF file.

5. Book Cover: You are given two options for cover submissions:-

i) Use the KDP free cover design tool, Cover Creator, to create your own cover;

ii) Upload your own print-ready PDF cover file;

iii) If your cover has a bar code tick the check box before upload. If the box is not ticked, KDP will add a bar code.

6. Book Preview: By clicking the 'Launch previewer' button this will open the online previewer where you can check your book to make sure it is the way you want it. If there are any formatting or layout errors these will be listed and you can rectify any issues which have been highlighted. The tasks you need to do are as follows:-

i) Check each page of the book;

ii) Check all page numbers and headings are in the correct place;

iii) Make sure numbering starts at page one of the story, not at page one of the front matter;

iv) Check the numbering stops on the last page of the story and does not continue into the back matter although, if it does, this is not a crucial issue;

v) Check that Chapter One starts on an odd numbered page.

vi) Check your cover to ensure nothing is distorted or cut off and that the bar code is in the correct place;

vii) If you find any issues, correct them in your manuscript or cover and re-upload the revised file.

If everything is correct, click 'Approve'. Then click 'Save and Continue'. You can now order a proof copy which may take between 5 to 10 days to arrive. The button for this is at the bottom of the 'Pricing' screen.

Paperback Rights & Pricing

1. Territories: Select the territories where you hold the distribution rights:

    i) If no one else has publishing or distribution rights, select 'All territories (worldwide rights)';

    ii) If there is any country where you do not hold the distribution rights, click the 'Individual territories' button and select the territories where you do hold the rights.

2. Pricing & Royalty:-

    i) Primary Marketplace: This is set for Amazon.com but you can change it to make Amazon.co.uk your primary marketplace. You can set your price so that it will automatically convert to the currency of the other marketplaces. The disadvantage of this is that currency conversion rates can vary from day to day which will cause fluctuations in the price of your book in all marketplaces except your primary one. Alternatively, you can set each marketplace with an individual price which will remain fixed;

    ii) Expanded Distribution: Tick this box if you wish to enable 'Expanded Distribution'. However, there are issues in respect of opting for this which I will discuss in the next section. In the meantime do not choose 'Expanded Distribution' if you intend to publish with IngramSpark for your UK books;

    iii) If you have not already done so, tick the box to order a proof copy. This may take between 5 to 10 days to arrive and it will have 'Proof' written on the cover.

Congratulations, you have now completed the process to publish your book with KDP.

You can now click 'Save as Draft' while you wait for your proof copy to arrive. Or you can click 'Publish Your Paperback Book'.

Issues in respect of expanded distribution

By selecting expanded distribution to bookstores and retailers KDP will submit your title to the Ingram database, which can prove problematic if you later want to use IngramSpark to publish your book.

Expanded distribution by KDP will make your book available to certified resellers such as independent bookstores and book resellers. It allows these resellers to buy books at wholesale prices directly from KDP. Resellers may then advertise your book at a horrendously high price on Amazon, but it doesn't mean they have your book in stock. All it means is that if anyone is foolish enough to pay more for your book than it is selling on Amazon, the reseller will simply buy it from KDP to fulfil the order, and you will not benefit from the higher price.

The other issue is that booksellers in general, including the aforementioned independent bookstores, are unlikely to buy books from KDP because it is an Amazon company. This means there is no benefit to be gained from opting for expanded distribution.

A word of warning! If you intend to publish your book, now or in the future, using IngramSpark, do not select the Expanded Distribution options.

Tip

Ordering multiple proof copies can be expensive particularly if you want priority delivery. I usually order my first proof from KDP and if I am reasonably happy with it but have to make some minor changes, I submit the revised book file, approve it for publication, and wait for Amazon to tell me it is published. Then I order a copy from the Amazon website and use that as my second proof.

16

Publishing to IngramSpark

IngramSpark

Unlike KDP, you cannot upload a formatted Word file to IngramSpark. You will require a PDF with embedded fonts and a single page layout. If the fonts are not embedded the file will be rejected.

Some writers use design software, such as Adobe InDesign, to lay out their manuscript in a format suitable for a paperback book, but unless you possess this software and are adept at using it, this could be a steep learning curve. Likewise, setting it out in a Word document requires you to become knowledgeable about sizes, margins, and gutters. It is far easier to layout a book using the correct size of KDP template and following the instructions on how to do this successfully. There are also paperback templates you can buy online but the KDP ones are free to use.

Assuming you have your book laid out as a paperback using a template, you will first have to change the spread from double page to single page. This is quite simple to do by changing 'Print Layout' to 'Normal' in Word's 'View' menu. You also need to check that 'Embed True Type Fonts' is ticked in the Options menu. And do not forget to add metadata to your Word file. Full instructions on how to do this are included in chapter nine, 'Formatting a Word document for Kindle'.

Microsoft Word has the ability to save a document as a PDF, however, on the PDF file checklist issued by IngramSpark, it states that "*PDFs created using the 'save as' function from MS Word are not supported*". I have Nuance PDF Power, the Standard version on my computer, and it puts a Create PDF menu inside Word. Here is how I do it but if you are using different PDF creation software the steps might be different.

If you do not have PDF conversion software there are several free options you can download from the internet, such as, PDF Creator, and CutePDF. Ensure the software you choose has the ability to embed fonts.

Remember, you need to change your KDP formatted file for your paperback into a single page spread. As I explained before, IngramSpark won't accept double page spreads.

1. Open the Word document of your book which you have formatted using the template.

2. Font embedding options:-

   a) PC – Click the 'File' tab, then in the sidebar menu click on 'Options'. In the window that opens click 'Save' to take you to the save options, then tick the box beside 'Embed Fonts in File'. Click 'OK' and then save your Word file to make sure the change applies to it.

   b) Mac – There is no option to embed fonts in Word for Mac, therefore this should be done when creating your PDF.

3. If you haven't already done so, change the page view from 'Print Layout' to 'Normal'.

4. Prior to using 'Create PDF' in your PDF program, go into PDF Settings and then Advanced Settings. Tick 'Embed Metadata' and then click 'Advanced' and then the 'PDF Settings' tab. Select 'Embed all Fonts' and then save.

If you are using different PDF software consult the manual or instructions, failing that do a Google search on how to embed fonts using your specific software.

5. Go back and click 'Create PDF'.

6. Wait for the PDF to be created and then save it.

There is an easy way to check whether or not the fonts in your PDF are embedded.

1. Open Adobe Reader (Acrobat Reader).

2. Open the PDF file of your book.

3. Click 'File', and then 'Properties'.

4. Click the 'Fonts' tab and it will display all your fonts with either 'Embedded' or 'Embedded Subset' after the name of the font. If any of the fonts do not have this after their name, the font is not embedded.

If you are successful and you now have a PDF file of your book, it is ready to be submitted.

Submission details

IngramSpark requires you to make more decisions than KDP does during the submission process.

Similar to KDP you will be asked to choose the size of your book, whether the interior should be black and white or colour (only choose colour if you are including colour illustrations. Black and white is the correct choice for a text only book). Then choose whether you want white or cream paper. In the UK cream is preferable for fiction, white for nonfiction.

The differences also relate to the type of book you require – paperback, hardcover, or ebook.

Assuming you choose paperback you will then be asked to choose binding type, eg perfect bound (bound with hot glue applied to the spine) or saddle stitched (bound with staples applied to the spine). Unless the book is very short, perfect bound is the best choice.

And finally, the laminate type for your cover. You have a choice of laminated gloss or matte, or cloth which is not laminated.

It is a good idea to have everything to hand that you will need to complete your submission and upload your file to IngramSpark. You will need:-

1. Your credit card and ISBN number;

2. The PDF file of your book;

If you plan to submit an ebook as well as a print version you will also need an epub file with no interactive elements, eg live links;

3. A brief description of the book plus a book jacket blurb;

4. A PDF book cover image for the print book plus a JPEG image for your ebook cover;

5. An author bio;

6. A list of your previous publications.

Create IngramSpark account

1. Go to www.ingramspark.com and click the 'Create New Account' button, then click 'Let's Get Started'.

2. Enter your email address and create a password.

3. Enter the type of business. For a self-publishing author, the most likely choice will be 'sole proprietorship'.

4. Answer a security question.

5. An email with an account activation will be sent to you. Click the link to activate your account.

6. On IngramSpark's home page use your email address and password to log in.

7. Accept the 'Terms of Use' and 'Privacy Policy'.

8. You will be prompted to review four agreements. The first two are required to confirm the agreement for IngramSpark to produce your titles. The other two are optional and you are probably best not to confirm these unless you want IngramSpark to distribute your ebooks to Apple and Kindle. If you confirm the last two options you will not be able to use KDP or any other distributor to sell your ebooks.

9. Once you complete these steps you will land on the

IngramSpark page where you can click the 'Visit Dashboard' button and take a video tour of the dashboard or you can click the 'Finish Setting Up My Account' button to complete the set up.

Financial Information

1.Complete Publisher Compensation: Click this link on your Dashboard and fill in the details to indicate the currency and how you prefer to receive payments eg bank account or Paypal.

2. Add Publisher Payment: Click this link to set up how you intend to pay for setup fees and print runs. Save the debit or credit card details.

3. Enter Tax Information: Click this link to provide your federal taxpayer ID. If you are outside the US, select the country you are located in and provide the required tax information.

Where applicable, IngramSpark will generate a W-9 form for you to review. If there are any errors, click the 'W-9 is not correct' button and fix the errors. Once all information is correct, click the confirmation button. Your account is now completely set up and you're ready to go.

Book Upload

Click the 'Add New Title' button on your Dashboard or under the 'Titles' tab to begin.

About Your Book page

1. Select Product Type: You have three choices. Print and Ebook, Print Only, Ebook Only. Select the one which applies.

There is an upload fee of $49 for print and $25 for ebooks. If you upload a print and ebook at the same time the fee is $49. However, if you order a print run of 50 copies of the print book within 60 days of uploading the title, IngramSpark will issue a $49 credit. If you are a member of ALLi (Alliance of Independent Authors) their discount will qualify you for free upload.

2. Title: The title of your book. If your book has a subtitle do not include it here.

3. Subtitle: Enter your subtitle here or leave blank.

4. Language: The language your book is written in.

5. Short Description: Brief summary of your book's content in a maximum of 350 characters.

6. Keywords: Enter up to 7 keywords or keyword phrases separated by semicolons, eg romance, crime, suspense etc.

7. Series Name and Number: Enter the name of the series and the number of the book in the series, otherwise leave blank.

8. Edition Description: If this is the first version of your book enter 1st edition. You will only ever need to enter 2nd edition if you substantially revise your book, or change the format etc which requires you to assign a new ISBN.

9. Full Description: Copy and paste the blurb from the back cover of your book. You are allowed between 200 to 4,000 characters (spaces are counted as characters). However, you will be unable to proceed any further until there are at least 200 characters in this space. Click 'Continue'.

About the Author/Contributors page

1. Contributors: Enter the last name of your author name first, then the first name and middle initial (if you have one and if you use it as part of your author name). This is the name that will be listed as the author of the book in Ingram's database and distribution network. Then click the 'About Contributors' button.

2. Biography: This is where you put your author bio, and it is preferable to keep it brief.

3. Prior work: If you have previously published other titles, list them here.

4. Location: If you identify with a particular area enter your location here.

5. Affiliations: List any organizations, agencies, schools, or nonprofits you're associated with. Click 'Continue'.

Categorize Your Book page

1. Imprint: Publishers often print their books under different imprints, for example, Picador is an imprint of Macmillan, and Avon is an imprint of Harper Collins. If you have decided to print your books using an imprint name, enter this here. Your imprint will then be listed by IngramSpark as the business name associated with your account.

2. Subjects: Click the 'Find Subjects' button. Type a simple classification such as 'fiction' in the search bar. A list of possible genres will be generated for you to choose from. If nothing matches, try another keyword to search. You can apply up to three classifications for your book, though you are only required to choose one. However, the more subjects you use to classify your books the more frequently it will come up in searches.

3. Regional Subject: If your book is set in a particular region of the world you can search for the locality.

4. Audience: If your book is not marketed to a particular age range it is best to default to adult/general.

5. Table of Contents: This is usually helpful for nonfiction, but is not necessary for fiction. If you have a Table of Contents, copy and paste it here.

6. Review Quotes: A brief excerpt rather than the full text of reviews by people who have given you permission to use

them.

7. Illustrations/Photographs: Confirm whether the book contains images or not. If there are images you must specify how many there are, and whether they are black and white or colour. Click 'Continue'.

Print Format page 1

1. Trim Size: Choose the size from the drop down menu. Popular sizes in the UK are 5 x 8 inches, and 5.5 x 8.5 inches.

2. Interior Color and Paper: Select Black and white for a fiction book with no images or illustrations. Color (IngramSpark spelling) is only applicable if you are publishing a book containing images. Paper colour for a fiction book in the UK is usually cream.

3. Binding Type: Select perfect bound for a paperback, and either case bound or cloth bound for a hardback.

4. Laminate Type: Choose either gloss or matte.

5. Stamped Text: This is only applicable for hardbacks where you want the title and author name stamped on the spine in gold letters.

6. Page Count: Enter the number of pages which should include front matter and back matter and any blank pages. One sheet of paper, back and front, counts as two pages. Your final page count must be an even number which is greater than 18 pages and less than 1,200 pages and the final page must be blank. Click 'Continue'.

Print Format page 2

1. Print ISBN: Enter your book's ISBN here. Be sure to use the same ISBN on all sales channels to avoid confusing retailers. Do not use a different ISBN for a book printed by KDP and the same book printed by IngramSpark. Of course, in order to do this, you must have bought your own ISBN and you

must remember to ensure the ISBN is added to the Nielsen (UK) database.

2. Pricing: Enter the retail price for the countries listed.

3. Choose the wholesale discount. The trade standard is 55% although you can choose a different rate. Bear in mind that unless you are extremely lucky and there is a high demand for your book, it is unlikely that retail stores will buy it in bulk. It is more likely their orders will be specifically for a customer requesting your book. If you wish to assign a lower discount rate, select 'Other' from the drop-down menu and enter a discount percentage.

4. Returnable: Bookstores normally expect to buy books on a sale or return basis and you have three options here.

    i) Yes – Deliver: Returned books will be shipped to the default mailing address on your IngramSpark Account;

    ii) Yes – Destroy: Returned books will be pulped and you will be billed by your distributor for the profit you made on the original sale of that book;

    iii) No: Retailers will not be allowed to return unsold copies of this title. Bear in mind what I said previously about the likelihood of bookstores stocking your book when making up your mind about this option, plus the fact that returns could wipe out any profit you make and could actually result in a loss.

5. Compensation: This is the profit you will make on each sale and is auto-generated when you enter the selling price of your book. The compensation is based on the retail price and wholesale discount. Payments are remitted within 90 days of the month-end reporting period following the sale.

6. Publication Date: The official release date of your book. Allow time for proofing and revising.

7. On Sale Date: The date retailers are allowed to sell your book or take orders for it. Click 'Continue'.

Ebook Format page

This section is only applicable if you are also publishing your ebook through IngramSpark.

1. Ebook ISBN: The digital edition of your ebook requires a different ISBN to the one on your print book because it is in a different format.

2. Pricing: Enter your list price for each regional market listed. It is worth noting that if you have chosen to allow IngramSpark to distribute to Apple, that the dollar retail price should always end in 99 cents (eg $3.99, $4.99 etc).

3. Distribution Rights: If you own the rights to sell anywhere in the world you should select 'Yes', otherwise select the regions you can sell it in. Click 'Continue'.

Title Files page

This page is divided into two columns for you to upload your files. The left-hand column is where you upload the interior and cover files for your print book, and the right-hand column is for the ebook files. Browse your computer for the relevant files and either select the files, or drag and drop them into the appropriate place, to upload.

The upload page is for two files or four files (PDF files for a print book, epub and JPEG for an ebook) depending on whether you are uploading print or ebook files only, or whether you are uploading for both versions. Don't forget that the PDF file for the interior of the print book should be on a single page spread with embedded fonts.

Click 'Continue'. You will be prompted to pay your upload fee which is $49. If you have one, enter your ALLi discount code and the fee page will appear with a zero amount. Your files will then be scanned for errors or glitches. If you have to amend and re-upload your files there is a revision fee of $25. This does not apply to members of ALLi (Alliance of Independent Authors) who are eligible for a discount code. If you are a member of

ALLi do not forget to enter this code otherwise you will be charged.

Once your files are print ready you will be sent an e-proof to approve. Following this, your book is ready to publish, although I would advise you to order one print copy to proof before ordering greater amounts.

Book orders

You can order books through the 'Create New Order' on your IngramSpark Dashboard, but before you order larger quantities it is recommended that you order one copy in order to check the book has been published to your satisfaction.

Once you are satisfied with the proof copy you can order a larger quantity. If you have more than one title with IngramSpark you can order different titles on the same order. If you have a promo code do not forget to enter it to receive the appropriate discount. (ALLi members can claim discounts).

Select your preferred printing speed; standard is five business days, expedited is two business days for express, or one day for a rush order. You will pay a slightly higher printing cost for expedited printing speeds. Shipping costs are calculated on weight, speed and location. However, my own experience has been that orders are usually delivered within 3 working days using standard shipping.

17

KDP and IngramSpark Combined

Kindle Direct Publishing and IngramSpark

Many authors in the UK combine publication by both KDP and IngramSpark. They use KDP to supply the Amazon market and IngramSpark for their UK books and distribution to all other markets.

If you wish to publish using both companies the process is the same as has been previously described, however, there are some things you have to watch out for.

1. Do not activate 'Expanded Distribution' in KDP.

2. Do not select 'distribute to Amazon' in IngramSpark.

Why are these two things important? And what can you do if they are already selected?

If Expanded Distribution is ticked in KDP and you then decide at a later stage you would like to use IngramSpark to publish your books, an error will be generated when you enter your ISBN in the IngramSpark Dashboard. You will get a message saying your ISBN is already in use. Your first reaction might be to think that is impossible. After all, you bought and paid for the ISBN, and you are listed as the publisher. But the reason for this is simple. KDP use Ingram for their Expanded Distribution, and that means your book is already in the Ingram database.

There are some ways around this. First, you have to pull your books from Expanded Distribution by turning this option off in your KDP account. However, that does not necessarily mean your book will immediately be removed from the Ingram database. There are varying estimates about how long it will take for this removal to take place – probably up to six weeks. You could also contact KDP to ask them to remove your book from the Ingram database if you want a faster result.

On the other hand, if you are still getting the ISBN in use message from IngramSpark they will send an agreement for you to sign to free the ISBN. The agreement they ask you to sign commits you to paying IngramSpark for any book returns that are made. It is safe enough to sign this agreement because KDP does not have a returns policy. I cannot guarantee the same for other self-publishing companies so you would have to check this.

If you select distribution to Amazon during the account setup process with IngramSpark, that will result in books being supplied from two different distributors which will be confusing if nothing else. I suggest you do not choose this option in the first place, and if you have already chosen it then you should deselect it.

If you plan to use more than one company to publish, print or distribute your book, it is essential you buy your own ISBN. If you take a free one, then it remains the property of whoever purchases it, effectively making them your publisher, and you cannot use that ISBN with any other company or printer. If you have already taken the free ISBN and have to buy an additional ISBN to allow your books to be published or printed elsewhere, this creates confusion for distribution because it results in two identical books with different ISBNs, and, as I previously explained, the ISBN is an identification number for the distributors and retail trade which they use to ensure they are buying the correct product.

18

Financial Considerations

Royalties

The KDP royalty for a 300-page paperback selling at £9.99 in the UK from the Amazon store is approximately £2.27. This is considerably more than the 8% (or if you are lucky 10%) you would earn from a traditional publisher.

Pricing your book

When pricing your paperback, the temptation is to make it as cheap as possible. This can be a big mistake and lead to losses at the point of sale.

There are other aspects than simply the difference between the cost price and the sale price to consider. Bookstores and distributors expect a discount and this can be as high as 60% unless you negotiate a better rate eg my discount rate with the main distributors is 30% which I negotiated. However, Waterstones require a massive 50% which I can only do if I hand deliver the books to the store.

The other cost to factor in when pricing your books is postage. Depending on the thickness of the book, an individual copy will cost either £2.05, or £2.85 to post, although slimmer volumes may cost less.

KDP

Unlike Createspace where all costs were in US dollars, KDP allows you to choose the currency you wish to use for buying and selling your books which means the costs of buying and selling are no longer dependent on the pound to dollar exchange rate.

Examples for a book selling on Amazon at £9.99 supplied by KDP:-

> KDP sale royalty = £2.27 (60% of the list price minus the publishing cost).

> Author copy cost price of a 300-page book = £3.72 + add 54p for standard shipping or 97p for expedited shipping per book for orders of 10 books. Total cost per book is £4.26 with standard shipping or £4.69 with expedited shipping. Shipping costs will vary according to the number of books ordered.

Examples for a book selling elsewhere at £9.99.

> Sales to a Distributor – price paid to you, less the 30% negotiated discount, equals £7.00. Your profit margin is the cost of your author copy plus postage, subtracted from the sales price.

> Sales to Waterstones – price paid to you, less the 50% discount, equals £5.00.

Bookstores and distributors work on a sale or return agreement. If you are asked to authorize the return of unsold books this can leave you seriously out of pocket. Not only will you be responsible for refunding the buyer but you will also have to pay for the shipping.

The protection against this is that you can argue POD books are special orders. But to ensure full protection include a phrase similar to this on your invoices 'All sales final. No sale or return policy'.

Selling your book with KDP

This is dependent on your choice of ISBN.

If you opted for the free KDP ISBN then your selling market is Amazon, apart from any copies you hand-sell.

KDP expanded distribution gives you access to bookstores and online retailers. If you are based in the US it also gives you access to US libraries and academic institutions. This all sounds very grand but in reality does not amount to much.

Booksellers are averse to buying from Amazon and unless your book is an academic one or a book that is in high demand, it is doubtful if it will be requested by these institutions. I could count on the fingers of one hand the number of expanded distribution sales I've made on Amazon.

It does make your book available to resellers, however, and I'm sure you've seen these in abundance on Amazon web pages selling books for exorbitant amounts. Or, if you click on the used and new offers on a book page, you will get a selection of prices. I currently have prices between £9.83 up to £53 on the reseller page of my latest book which Amazon sell for £9.99. But if anyone is foolish enough to pay £53 to a reseller for this book it won't make any difference to the amount paid to me.

If you buy your own ISBN and are therefore the publisher of the book, your main selling market is still Amazon.

However, Nielsen will send order lines to you when your book is requested by a distributor or bookseller. It is your responsibility to respond to the request and provide the book, bearing in mind the issues in respect of finance, discussed above.

IngramSpark

IngramSpark allows you to choose the currency you wish to use for buying and selling your books, therefore, the costs of buying and selling are not dependent on the pound to dollar exchange rate. This means you always know what your costs will be.

IngramSpark is also a distributor and will fulfil orders to bookstores and retailers at the discount rate you choose.

Retailers will expect to buy on a sale or return basis with a 55% discount unless they are fulfilling special orders. A special order is a guaranteed sale therefore they will buy your book at a lesser discount and without a commitment for sale or return.

When you set your discount rate, bear in mind it is unlikely that retailers will order your books in any great numbers, and that the sales will probably be for special orders.

You can specify no sale or return on books sold which will protect you from making a loss. Returns can wipe out all your profit and more, so think carefully about this.

Examples for a 300-page book priced at £9.99, supplied by IngramSpark:-

Royalties

Royalty with a wholesale discount of 55% = 54 pence;

Royalty with a wholesale discount of 40% = £2.03;

Royalty with a wholesale discount of 30% = £3.03.

Costs (book plus handling plus shipping)

Costs = £3.96 per book plus a handling fee of £1.65 per order irrespective of order size;

Shipping cost for 1 copy = £3.16 = total cost per book £8.77;

Shipping costs for 10 books = £5.65 (approximately 56 pence per book) = total cost per book £4.69;

Shipping costs for 50 books = £12.23 (approximately 25 pence per book) = total cost per book £4.21.

Local booksellers may be interested in stocking your book so it is to your advantage to visit and discuss terms with them.

The other selling areas worth considering are craft fairs, book fairs, and community groups looking for a speaker. This is the most remunerative way to sell your books.

It is worth investing in promotional materials, such as postcards or bookmarks. These can be distributed at various venues or handed to readers interested in your books. If you are in demand for author talks, or if you appear at craft or book fairs, banners are an inexpensive way of catching the eye.

In Conclusion

As can be seen, the cost price of a book can vary according to the choices you make.

On balance, provided you select the standard shipping option, KDP paperbacks can work out slightly cheaper to produce although, if expedited shipping is required, the publication cost of a KDP book is similar to that of one produced by Ingram Spark.

However, there is a considerable difference in the delivery times of books dispatched by both companies.

Standard delivery from KDP can take between 10 to 19 days, while expedited delivery is slightly faster, taking between 7 to 8 days from the placing of an order.

Ingram Spark, on the other hand, has a faster delivery time frame.

My Ingram Spark orders have always been delivered within 3 working days using standard delivery. Ingram Spark delivery is so fast there is little point in requesting expedited delivery.

Royalties are more difficult to compare because it depends on the wholesale discount you choose with Ingram Spark. If you choose the maximum discount rate of 55% your royalty will be far less than the one you will receive from KDP. However, if you choose the lower 30% rate, then your royalty will be greater than that of KDP.

In terms of the quality of author copies there is very little difference. Both firms supply good quality books although I find that the Ingram Spark quality is slightly better.

If you find it difficult to make your mind up I would suggest placing an order with KDP and a similar order with Ingram Spark and make your own comparisons.

19

After Publication

Your book is published: What now?

You have pressed the button to publish your book and maybe you think there is nothing left to do but sit back and wait for the money to roll in.

But, wait a minute, who knows your book is out there? How do you find it among all the millions of books already on sale? Yes, you've guessed it, now is the time to market your book. But before you do that you have some legal responsibilities.

National Library and Legal Depository

There is a statutory requirement, embodied in law since 1662, for one copy of every UK publication to be deposited at the British Library and other designated deposit libraries.

The current legislation which applies is the Legal Deposit Libraries Act 2003 which applies to any person who publishes in the UK, and it stipulates that the Act covers the following – a book (including a pamphlet, magazine, or newspaper); a sheet of letterpress or music; a map, plan, chart or table; and a part of any such work.

Every new publication and every new edition of a book must be lodged, but it does not apply to reprints of the same book.

These publications become a research resource and are included in the deposit library's online catalogue for the availability of users who can inspect the books within the deposit library premises. They are not available to borrow.

The statutory responsibility for complying with the Act rests with the publisher, therefore if you are self-publishing your book and have purchased your own ISBN the responsibility is yours.

If you have taken a free ISBN from KDP, or another self-publishing print supplier the responsibility rests with them as your publisher.

Of course, if the ISBN is a KDP one, your book will not be lodged in the British Library or any of the other UK Legal Deposit libraries for posterity because KDP is not a UK publisher. Your book is effectively a US publication.

The legislation states, under Section 4, that the British Library must be sent one copy of your book within one month of publication. They do not request it but it is the publisher's responsibility to ensure this is done. If no copy is received they will send a notification to remind you of your statutory responsibility.

Section 5, of the legislation, states that each Legal Deposit library, other than the British Library, is also entitled to a copy of your book. But they must make this request. Therefore, you are under no obligation to send these copies until you receive this notification. When you receive the request you must deposit five copies with the Agency for the Legal Deposit Libraries which is currently situated in Edinburgh. Your response must be within one month of receipt of the request.

Do not make the mistake of combining the books for the British Library and the Agency for Legal Deposit in the same delivery. They work independently, therefore one book should be posted to the British Library, and five copies of the book shipped to the Agency for the Legal Deposit Libraries.

The Agency for the Legal Deposit Libraries services five libraries: the Bodleian Libraries of the University of Oxford; Cambridge University Library; the National Library of

Scotland; the Library of Trinity College, Dublin; and the National Library of Wales. One copy of your book will be deposited in each of those libraries.

Addresses

Legal Deposit Office, The British Library, Boston Spa, Wetherby, LS23 7BQ (send one book).

Agency for the Legal Deposit Libraries, 21 Marnin Way, Edinburgh, EH12 9GD (send 5 books when requested).

Legal Deposit In Other Countries

Legal deposit of publications is required in most countries although the conditions and number of copies vary from country to country.

In the US two copies must be deposited with the United States Copyright Office at the Library of Congress.

I suggest you explore the situation in your country of publication because this is a legal requirement.

Author pages

The next thing on your to do list, is to ensure you set up author pages on the sites where your books are published, for example, Smashwords and Amazon.

Your author page on Amazon is accessed by readers who click on the image of you on the page listing your books or lower on the page featuring a specific book. My one has the heading 'Chris Longmuir's Author Page'. Of course, if you haven't added a photograph of yourself it will simply display a placeholder.

As a reader, when I am considering a new author I will always click on the author page link, so it is quite important what you add to this page. It is a prime promotional opportunity.

Author Central operates on most Amazon sites, but they all operate independently so you have to add the details to every Author Central site in every country which sells your books. All Author Central sites provide the basic information for your author page. However, AuthorCentral.com is the only one which will allow you to edit the description of your book which is a quick and easy way to make changes.

Setting up Author Central

1. Sign into Amazon Author Central. Your password is the same for all your Amazon accounts.

2. On the Welcome to Author Central page click 'Books' at the top left. The books page will appear.

3. Click 'Add More Books'.

4. Enter either the title, author or ISBN in the 'Search' box. If you enter your name here all your books will come up in a dialog box along with their covers.

5. Click under each book you wish to add. Be careful, because sometimes your books which are being sold by resellers will appear in this dialog box as well. You do not wish to claim these books which are often advertised on Amazon for extortionate prices. If you do claim a reseller's copy of your book on Author Central that book will still be there when the reseller no longer features it and it will appear on the Amazon site as 'unavailable'. If a buyer only sees the reseller's copy of your book they may look no further. Therefore, only claim the books which are included in your own KDP account. After you add the books, close the dialog box.

6. Click on 'Profile' in the menu bar. Click 'Add Biography' enter the information. Do the same with any photos and videos you want on your page.

7. Add your blog, and your Twitter feed.

PLR and ALCS

The next thing you need to do is register for PLR (Public Lending Right) and ALCS (Authors' Licensing and Collecting Society).

PLR

PLR is short for Public Lending Right. Until fairly recently PLR funding was managed by the Registrar of Public Lending Right, but from 1 October 2013, the UK PLR office became part of the British Library.

On the British Library website, it says, "Public Lending Right (PLR) is the right for authors to receive payment for the loans of their books by public libraries."

This is governed by legislation, and payment is made from government funds. In order to be eligible for inclusion in the PLR scheme authors are required to register, but that is easily done either by post or online at the British Library PLR website www.plr.uk.com. You will find the conditions for registration on this website as well as a downloadable application form. The current payment rate is 8.2 pence per library loan.

However, in order to receive payments from the PLR scheme, it is not enough to have your books available for loan in a library because the PLR system works on the basis of statistics taken from a sample number of libraries. So, if your books are not available in any of the sample libraries, then your income will be nothing, irrespective of how popular your books are in other libraries. Now, I'm afraid this is where I have to admit that my understanding of statistics is abysmal. I have a creative brain rather than a logical mathematical one, so you can understand why statistics remain a mystery. So I will quote what the website says *"Payments are made annually on the basis of loans data collected from a sample of public libraries in the UK."* This sounds simple enough but when they mention how they gross-up the loans, I am lost. The best I can do is quote again, *"Because PLR loans are derived from a representative sample of library authorities, a grossing up calculation is applied to the actual loans at the end of each PLR reporting year, in order to provide a national estimate of loans for the whole of the UK and Ireland."*

To look further at book loans data. This is collected over a twelve month period, from 1 July to 30 June. For the purposes of this book, I am looking at payments for my own books based on the year July 2012 to June 2013, which was when I did the research. The payment for each loan at that time was the massive sum of 6.2 pence per loan, and a librarian friend told me that on average a reader will keep a book for a month, so that would work out at twelve loans per year. During that year I had 79 loans in Angus libraries for my two non-earning books, and I earned £8.18 for Dead Wood which originated from a library in Wales, otherwise this book would also have earned no PLR.

I did wonder why, in this technological age, the PLR system was based on statistical sampling, rather than collecting information from all libraries, but according to them this would be impracticable and expensive to do, although I don't quite see the rationale for this given the vast improvements in technology. However, the size of the sample has improved over the years. The 16 individual library branches in 1982 has now increased to 30 library authorities, with approximately 1,000 individual branches.

For the purposes of PLR, the country is divided up into regions into which library authorities are grouped. Each grouping may include between two to seven different library authorities. The libraries included for sampling have to be public libraries operating as part of the statutory library service, provided by local authorities. Community libraries, trusts, and those set up by independent groups are not included.

There are nine PLR sample regions in England, one in Scotland, one in Wales and one in Northern Ireland.

The current English PLR regions are East (two library authorities), London (seven library authorities), North East (two library authorities), North West and Merseyside (six library authorities), South East (two library authorities), South West (two library authorities), West Midlands (one library authority), Yorkshire and The Humber (one library authority). As you can see the majority of these regions cover several library authorities with London having the majority listed under London Libraries Consortium.

Scotland is a single PLR region with four library authorities, and because I live in Scotland I was interested in which library authorities were included. The grouping is, Aberdeenshire, Edinburgh, Highland, and Midlothian. Wales, also a single PLR region, has three local authorities included. But the one I found most interesting was Northern Ireland because the whole of Northern Ireland is included in the sample.

If you want to check the authorities included for 2015-2016 you can do so on the PLR website.

I checked back over previous years and discovered the last time Angus (my library authority) was included was the PLR sample year 1996-97 which was 20 years ago, and now that the libraries have become a trust in Angus it is unlikely it will ever be included again. Edinburgh and Glasgow are featured fairly regularly, although unlike London, they are not included every year. There is an archive of previous sample authorities at plr.uk.com.

That begs the question – how often do they change the sample authorities? Well, according to the website, at least seven of the library authorities are replaced each year, and no authority can stay in the sample longer than four years.

So there you have it. If you are lucky enough to live in one of the sampling authorities and the libraries in that authority stock your books, then you will get PLR payments. However, if like me, the reverse is the case, then I reckon you should not count on PLR as part of your writing income.

But, in conclusion, if you were to ask me whether it is beneficial to register for PLR in the knowledge you may get nothing, then my answer would be yes. You see, if an author does not register then this reduces the number of authors on the PLR database. Then, who knows, maybe a future decision could be that these payments are no longer necessary, and as a result, the scheme would be scrapped. So, I would encourage you to register.

Lastly, can I just say that if you like a specific writer's books and want to support them, then please put a request into your local library for their books, irrespective of whether you already have the paperback or kindle version. It will get the books onto the library shelves, and hopefully, they will be included in a sample, sooner or later.

How to register books for PLR

1. Apply for an online account or if you already have an account log in at www.plr.uk.com.

2. Click on the 'Add New' tab.

3. Fill in the following details:-

    i) ISBN;

    ii) Title: Name/Pseudonym (author name);

    iii) Publisher (publisher name or imprint name);

    iv) Publication year (year the book was first published);

    v) Edition Type (select from drop down list);

    vi) Your Percentage Share (this will be 100% unless you share authorship with someone else). I think I need to reinforce that 'your percentage share' is not the percentage share that you are entitled to after sales, nor is it the percentage share you receive from your publisher, your royalty. It is the percentage share of the book which is entitled to PLR and this will be 100% unless you have a co-author who requires a share. I fell into this trap myself when I was initially published and entered the royalty percentage instead of 100%.

4. In the column on the right-hand side of the form, select the appropriate description of your contribution to the book. If

you are a sole author and entitled to the 100% share, then you should tick 'Writer'.

5. Click 'Add books to table below' at the bottom right side of the form.

An email will be sent once the book is registered and it will be added to the table with all your registered books, under the 'approved registrations' tab.

ALCS

ALCS is short for Authors' Licensing and Collecting Society. It is a not-for-profit membership organization whose purpose is to collect secondary royalties on behalf of writers.

The society tracks secondary uses of members' work, such as photocopying, scanning, and digital copying.

They collect the money owed which they then pay to authors twice a year in February/March and August/September.

There is a single lifetime fee of £36 to become a member of ALCS but you do not have to pay this at the time of joining. The fee will be deducted from your first royalty payment.

However, if you are a member of the Society of Authors the fee is waived.

How to register for ALCs

Click 'Apply to join' on the ALCS website at alcs.co.uk. Alternatively download paper forms which you can fill in and post. Please note that only UK residents may apply online for membership, if you live overseas you will need to download the paper form and submit this by post.

Steps to complete:-

1. Personal details page: Name; writing name; date of birth; nationality. Click 'Next'.

2. How to Contact you page: Address; email; phone etc. Click 'Next'.

3. How Should we Pay You page: Select payment options click either 'to you' or 'to agent', then fill in bank details. Click 'Next'.

4. Communications from ALCS page: This is where you are asked how you heard about ALCS. Click 'Next'.

5. Do You have an Agent: Fill this in if you have an agent otherwise leave blank.

6. Are you registered for VAT: Leave blank unless you are VAT registered; tick any societies you are a member of or leave blank. Click 'Next'.

7. Confirm your Details page: Check your details and click 'Submit'.

Following completion, you will be emailed a copy of your application form which you must sign and return by post.

Reports

Traditionally published authors rely on royalty statements which are sent annually or twice a year on a specific date.

These reports are not usually easy to understand and the author is often left with a poor understanding of book sales and an inability to assess the success or otherwise of promotional activities.

Some of the more progressive publishers now have web-based author portals where the number of book sales can be checked.

However, due to their sale or return policies, the royalties they pay do not equate to sales because a percentage of a book's royalties is retained by the publisher to cover the cost of future returns eg unsold books returned by the retailers to the publisher.

The self-published author knows exactly how much income is being accrued from their book sales therefore they are better informed. Most self-publishing platforms supply reports which are easily understood.

The Kindle Direct Publishing (KDP) platform details sales in real time and it is possible to track sales as they occur day-to-day.

Likewise, Smashwords, and IngramSpark have reliable reporting systems. This is useful if you want to judge the effect of any promotional activity and allows you to see what works best.

Business Aspects

This is probably the time to set up your accounting systems if you haven't done it already. There are various accounting software programs you can buy, but my accountant prefers simple excel spreadsheets.

I set up two spreadsheets, one for income and one for expenditure. In each spreadsheet, I set up columns to separate out the different types of income and the different types of expenditure.

I like to know where my main income is coming from, ebooks or paperbacks, as well as anything I earn from speaking events. Likewise with expenditure. This is broken down into publishing costs, travel, office supplies, postage, research, and promotion and marketing.

The tax man will expect you to send in a self-assessment tax return for each financial year.

This is something you can either do yourself or engage an accountant to do for you. Frankly, I think an accountant will save you money and they are well worth the fee you pay them.

If you continually register a loss, over a six year period, the tax authorities may reclassify you as a hobby writer.

Promotion and Marketing

This is something you have to think about irrespective of whether you are traditionally published or self-published. Your publisher will not promote your book unless you are already a best-selling author.

The problem is that no one knows what really works and what doesn't. But there are things you can do, such as have a website, a blog, post on Twitter, Facebook, Pinterest, Instagram, and anywhere else you can think of. But the thing to avoid is inundating people with 'buy my book' posts.

The aim is to build a platform and get your name known. And remember, what worked in the past may not necessarily work now.

The latest things have been podcasts and webcasts, but even these are becoming less effective as more and more people jump on the bandwagon. But there is one thing I think does work and that is the email list of your fans.

Advice on promotion and marketing is beyond the scope of this book. However, I have included details of some publications on this topic in the references and resources section at the end of this book.

Metadata

There is no need to shudder when you see metadata described as something you need to think of in order to boost sales. Metadata is simply a word to describe the search terms readers use to find your book. For example, I might do a search for 'romance novels', or 'spy thrillers', or 'murder mystery'. If your metadata indicates this is the kind of book you write it will come up in the searches. However, the most popular books in these categories will head the list that comes up.

But there is a caveat. If a genre is popular there are more potential results and therefore it is less likely your book will show high enough in the results for searchers to notice. For example, 'romance' has 1,225,829 results, while spy thrillers have 24,666. But if you hone your metadata to something more specific, you can lessen the number of results that show, eg 'oriental romance' has 723 results, a tiny fraction of the 'romance' category.

To use metadata, you include it in the tags on your Amazon upload page, and you include them in your book description. Of course, you have to do it sensibly weaving them into the description in a realistic way.

Professional Associations

The main two professional associations are:-

ALLi (Alliance of Independent Authors) and the Society of Authors.

There are several other professional associations for writers, some of which are genre based, although not all of them are open to self-publishing authors. Among the other associations are the Historical Novel Society (HNS), the Romantic Novelist Society (RNA), as well as most of the other genres. An internet search is the best way to find the association related to your genre.

The Society of Authors (SOA)

Most workers have organizations which look after their interests and provide an element of protection in their chosen field of work. Many have unions that provide this protection, while others have professional associations. Writers are no different.

The main professional association for writers in the UK is the Society of Authors (SOA) which also acts as a union.

The SOA will act in an author's interests in many ways.

In the wider sense, it will lobby parliament and fight for better conditions such as promoting payment for all speaking appearances and events. For too long many conference and event organizers have expected authors to appear for no payment, but this is changing, thanks to the SOA.

On a smaller scale, the SOA will vet publisher contracts and provide advice and assistance to any author experiencing difficulties.

In my case, they were instrumental in helping me to reclaim the publishing rights to my books after they went out of print.

Membership criteria

There are two levels of membership – Associates and Members both of which are open to traditionally published and self-published writers who meet the criteria set.

Associates are those writers who are at an early stage of their career, while Members are established, professional authors.

1. Members:-

    i) A member working professionally will require to have had a full-length work traditionally published, broadcast, or performed commercially. Or, have published a body of work eg articles, short stories, poems, or items in other media.

    ii) Established self-publishers who have sold over 300 copies of a single title in print form or 500 copies in ebook form within a 12 month period.

2. Associates:-

    i) Writers who have received an offer to publish or broadcast a full-length work in any format, or have an agency agreement with a UK agent but have had no work published.

    ii) Writers starting to self-publish but have not yet begun to make a profit.

Alliance of Independent Authors (ALLi)

Indies or self-publishers also have access to an organization which protects their interests. The Alliance of Independent Authors (ALLi).

There are four membership categories:-

1. Author Member: You have published or self-published a book.

2. Professional Author: You have sold more than 50,000 books.

3. Partner Member: You are a business or freelance providing author services.

4. Associate Author: You are preparing a book for self-publishing.

Other professional organizations

Crime Writers Association (CWA): Membership of the CWA is open to traditionally published crime writers, and provisional membership is available for those crime writers with a publishing contract but who have not yet been published. It is not currently open to self-publishers, nor if you have paid to be published.

Romantic Novelists Association (RNA): Full Membership is open to traditionally published authors of romantic novels and full-length serials: Independent Author Membership is open to self-published writers.

Historical Novel Society (HNS): Membership is open to everyone irrespective of country, reading preference, or publishing history.

20

My Own Experience

My experience of the indie world of self-publishing

It is my earnest hope that this guide to self-publishing has proved useful and for those of you who are interested in my own experience of the self-publishing world, I have included this here.

My experience of self-publishing has been gained through a process of trial and error and I have written this book to share with you the knowledge I have acquired along the way.

My first book, the crime novel Dead Wood, was published in the traditional way after winning the prestigious international book prize for debut novelists, the Dundee International Book Prize.

What an exciting time that was. But the procedure prior to publication was not without pain.

Any author will tell you that writing 'The End' on the last page, is not really the end. There follows a period which can last up to a year or even longer, but in my case was eight months, for the editorial process.

During this time conflicting demands were made – I had to add words and cut words. The cover was decided by the publisher and the title was changed.

But what a feeling of achievement there was when I held my book in my hands and saw it on the bookstore shelves with my name on the cover.

Now, all of the above may seem fairly easy to the new author, but that book had been hawked around publishers and agents for four years prior to winning the prize. Rejections were the order of the day. The last rejection I had was one month before winning the prize, and that publisher had retained the book for four years before making up his mind.

So, two years after Dead Wood was published, after going through the same frustrating process of trying to interest publishers and agents in my second book, Night Watcher, I decided to go down the electronic route and publish to Kindle.

Apart from the formatting it was a relatively painless process, and it cost me nothing except for the editing fee which was a good investment.

Shortly after publishing to Kindle I published the book to Smashwords, an ebook distributor, so that readers could access my novel on other devices such as the Sony Reader, Kobo, Nook, and the Apple iPad.

Admittedly, I did not have that wonderful feeling of holding a book in my hands, but at least it was out there and being read. After all, what is a writer without readers?

After I published Night Watcher as an ebook I started to see how much the publishing world was changing. Electronic publishing was now much more prominent than it was when I first became published and as I was now an author who had published both ways it seemed to me a good time to weigh up the pros and cons.

So what are the pros and cons?

Well, with traditional publishing there is all the pain of constant rejections plus the length of time everything takes. With e-publishing, the book can be on sale almost immediately, although I would advise sending it to a literary agency or editor prior to taking that step. A traditional publisher may pay 8 per cent royalties for print books and between 15 to 20 per cent for ebooks (average), while the self-publisher can earn between 35 to 85 per cent for ebooks. But best of all you are independent.

The feeling of liberation is marvellous because you do not have to prostrate yourself to publishers.

I would say the e-publishing route has been a success for me, although I did miss being able to hold my book following publication.

This was one of the reasons I decided to dip my toe into the paperback publishing waters, and now have paperbacks of my novels as well as ebooks.

Adventures with self-publishing

When I decided to publish with Createspace which was long before its move to KDP print, I had been publishing Kindle ebooks with a reasonable amount of success and with great satisfaction.

Like many others, before me, I had come to the conclusion, that by pursuing a traditional deal with a traditional publisher, I was flogging, if not a dead horse, then certainly one not in the best of health, and I had embarked wholeheartedly into the wonders of the electronic world of ebooks.

So, once I became part of the electronic world, what on earth would induce me to return to the print world?

Well, my original decision stood – I had decided I was done with the traditional route to publishing my books.

However, I am often asked to talk to various readers' groups. I visit libraries, speak at conferences, do adjudications, and take an active role in professional writers' societies, such as the Society of Authors and the CWA (Crime Writers' Association). One thing that arose every time I gave a talk was, *"Where can we get the paperback?"* And I always had to say, *"There is no paperback. Have you thought about getting an eReader?"* And that often came back with a resounding, *"No, we like paper books."*

Eventually, I gave in. My readers were demanding paperbacks, so it was my job to provide them.

Now, I knew that if I went back down the traditional route, the publisher would want my electronic rights as well. And that is something I did not want to surrender. I am determined not to relinquish my electronic rights. So that left only one avenue, self-publishing.

Like a lot of authors before me I had to battle against the idea that there was a stigma attached to self-publishing, and I find many authors who still publish the traditional way can be among the most disapproving. They forget about the famous writers who were originally self-published. Writers like – Mark Twain, Zane Grey, William Blake, Virginia Woolf, James Joyce, D H Lawrence, Edgar Rice Burroughs, George Bernard Shaw, Edgar Allan Poe, and Rudyard Kipling. Even Jane Austen self-published three of her novels – I could go on and on.

Maybe part of my reluctance to go down the paperback route was partly to do with the thought of that stigma. Self-publishing on Kindle did not really seem like self-publishing in the true sense of the word, but if I published a paperback I would truly be a self-publisher.

My desire to satisfy my readers soon overcame that last vestige of reluctance and I looked around to see how I could do it. The one proviso I gave myself was that I would not pay for my book to be published because to me that smacked of vanity publishing, something with an even greater stigma. So I looked around the POD (print on demand) publishers and settled on Amazon's Createspace, although I had heard that having books shipped from the US was very expensive.

I found the procedure relatively simple by using one of the templates Createspace make available. I copied and pasted my book into the template, chapter by chapter, as per instructions, but the biggest decision at this point was the font. Which one would I use? I tried several but the ones I liked did not have curly quotes, and I do like them curly! So I came back to the tried and tested Times New Roman with a two point 'leading' which formats extra space between the lines. This enhances the reading experience because the text is not crammed together.

I did not take the advice of Createspace on the most popular format, because when I looked around my bookshelves I could not find any books that were size 6 x 9 with white pages. Books were mostly 8 x 5 inches or 8.5 x 5.5 inches, and they all had cream pages. I decided on the 8.5 x 5.5 size with cream pages, and the resulting book exceeded my expectations.

The next stage was to decide whether I wanted a Createspace ISBN which is supplied free, but it would have made Createspace the publisher. Now, being the independent person I am, otherwise known as an awkward sod, I decided I did not want to be beholden to CreateSpace, so I went the alternative route and bought my own ISBNs.

I particularly liked the Createspace digital reviewer, an online tool, which allows you to see how the actual book will look when it is published. I also found the downloadable PDF useful; this sets the manuscript out like a book. It made the inspection and proofing relatively easy. However, I did order a physical proof before approving the book.

Once my first book was on stream as a paperback I went ahead and did the same for the others. So now I have several paperback novels available as well as my Kindle versions, and the strange thing is, there has been an increase in Kindle sales since the paperbacks became available.

There was one other surprise. When I ordered my first twenty author copies from Createspace they came in cheaper than the author copies provided by my mainstream publisher. And that was despite the cost of postage from the US. However, I have never been able to understand why the Createspace author copies had to be dispatched from the US when customers buying them in this country are provided with UK copies. The mysteries of Amazon!

I did not have any great expectations from sales of my paperbacks which I only brought on as a service to my readers. However, sales have been better than I expected although ebook sales provide my main income.

It should be noted that over the past year Createspace has closed and has become part of Kindle Direct Publishing. The procedure to publish remains much the same although there have been some changes in the process. These changes have been incorporated in this book.

21

The Final Word

Thank you for reading this book which I decided to write following my successful nuts and bolts of self-publishing workshop at the Scottish Association of Writers conference. Prior to that, I had not considered writing a guide on self-publishing even though I am often asked for advice on a variety of self-publishing topics, which I gladly give. In fact, one of my contacts calls me his guru. But it was preparing for and delivering the nuts and bolts of self-publishing workshop that opened my eyes to the wealth of knowledge and experience I had gathered over the years. It has been my pleasure to share this knowledge with you and I hope it will help you in your quest for publication.

Finally, if you have found this book useful and would like to help others find this book as well, it would be great if you could find the time to write a short review on the website where you bought the book. It would be helpful to others who are considering the self-publishing path and I am sure they would appreciate it.

Chris Longmuir

Appendix One

Formatting Earlier Word Versions

Formatting a book for Kindle is quite easy, but the thing to bear in mind is that Microsoft Word has hidden formatting which can play havoc with your file during the conversion process.

So, before you follow the instructions to remove all formatting there are certain steps to go through to ensure that Microsoft Word doesn't replace all the formatting you've been at pains to remove.

This set of instructions refers to versions of Word which use the classic menu bar.

Preparing your Word document

You need to do this in a blank document prior to inserting your format free file, or before selecting the 'Clear Formatting' command in your current document, depending on which approach you use.

1. Open a new Word file.

2. Select 'Tools' in the Menu Bar, and from the drop down menu select 'AutoCorrect Options'. This will open the AutoCorrect dialog box.

3. Click on the 'AutoCorrect' Tab in the dialog box and remove the ticks from all boxes. Once you have done this the 'Auto Correct' box should have no ticks.

4. Click on the 'AutoFormat' tab at the top of the box. In the top section 'Apply' remove all ticks. In the next section 'Replace' remove all ticks except for 'Straight quotes' with 'Smart quotes', and 'Hyphens (--) with (–)'. It is safe to leave the bottom section 'Preserve' as it is.

5. Click on the tab 'AutoFormat As You Type'. All tick boxes should be empty except for the 'Straight quotes' and 'Hyphen' boxes, as above.

6. Click on the 'Smart Tags' tab and remove the tick from the box 'Label text with smart tags'. If you do find smart tags in your document you can remove them from here.

Step 1

Removing formatting from your Word document

There are two methods of removing the formatting in your Word document.

I will discuss the nuclear method first and then the alternative method which you can do from inside your original Word document.

You can remove the formatting from your file without going to the extreme of the nuclear approach. However, if you are having problems with your file after conversion, you may have to take it back to the beginning and do the nuclear option.

Always work with your formatting turned on in your menu bar (it looks like a backwards-facing P). If it's not in your menu bar click on the arrow at the end of the bar, the additional formatting icons are in there. This enables you to see paragraph returns, tabs, and any other formatting in your document.

Using the nuclear approach

Please note the nuclear approach is optional. However, it ensures your document is completely devoid of any of Microsoft's sneaky hidden formatting. But you must make sure you paste the resulting document into a new Word document with all the auto formatting and auto correct options switched off, otherwise Word will replace the formatting which has been removed.

1. Open your Word file. Delete all page numbers, headers, and footers.

2. Select 'Edit' from the menu bar, then click on 'Select All' from the drop down menu, alternatively, you can use the keystrokes CTL+A. This will select your entire document ready for the next stage.

3. Copy your entire document using the copy command or CTL+C. Close your Word file and keep this as a backup.

4. Open Windows Notepad. You'll find it in the 'All Programs; Accessories' on your computer, which you access from the Windows 'Start' button in the taskbar. Or you can use any other text editor, but not Word.

5. Paste your document into Notepad using the paste command, CTL+V. This will strip all the formatting out and you will have a plain text document.

6. Open Microsoft Word so that it is showing a new document, making sure you've turned off all the auto-formatting as described in the previous section, because if you don't, Word will put in all the hidden formatting again!

7. In Notepad select all your text using the keystrokes CTL+A, then copy it CTL+C, and paste it into your clean Word document CTL+V. You now have your clean Word document minus all formatting.

A word of caution! I sometimes find a rogue tab in the document after this process, so it is worth doing a search for Tabs using Word's Find and Replace box. You can find the symbol for tabs in the Find box if you click on 'More', and then on 'Special'.

Now you are ready to format your document prior to the kindle conversion.

Using the alternative approach

Please note the nuclear approach described above is optional and you can strip the formatting using this alternative process. Remember to turn off all the AutoCorrect and AutoFormat options in your file first. If this approach results in errors or glitches in your converted file you may then have to consider reformatting using the nuclear approach.

Always work with your formatting turned on (it looks like a backwards-facing P). If it's not in your menu bar click on the arrow at the end of the bar and you will find that the additional formatting icons are in there. This enables you to see paragraph returns, tabs, and any other formatting in your document.

1. Open your Word file. Delete all page numbers, headers, and footers.

2. Select 'Edit' from the menu bar, then 'Select All' from the drop down menu, alternatively, you can use the keystrokes CTL+A. This will select your entire document ready for the next stage.

3. Select 'Format', then select 'Styles and Formatting' from the drop down menu. Depending on your version of Windows you will either get a dialog box that opens or a strip down the side of your Document window. Mine is the latter.

4. Select 'Clear Formatting'.

This strips all the formatting from your document. You can miss this step if you are sure you do not have any fancy formatting in your document, no tabs, and no space bar spacing to make tabs etc, but I wouldn't advise it.

5. Make sure any further formatting to your document remains based on 'Normal' in the menu bar. Check the document for any tabs that have not been removed. They need to be deleted.

Step 2

Reformatting the document

After you have removed all formatting from your document you will be left with plain text with no formatting at all. If you are sure you are working with a clean file you can start to reformat the text. All new formatting should be based on 'Normal', and you must ensure you are working from 'styles' which you access from the drop down menus. Do not be tempted to format using the icons on the menu bar.

The instructions are for an indented prose style.

1. Click on 'Select All' in the 'Edit' menu or press CTL+A on the keyboard to highlight your document.

2. Click on the 'Format menu', then select 'Paragraph' from the drop down menu. The paragraph styling box will open.

3. Select the following in the paragraph box:-

   i) Alignment: 'Left'.

   ii) Special: 'First Line' – 'By' '0.5' – (Smashwords prefers 0.3 in this box. So do I). These sizes are in inches. If your measurements are metric, simply convert them to the metric equivalent.

   iii) Line Spacing: 'Single'. It is important to make sure that there is absolutely nothing in the 'At' box, as apparently, this can really mess up your document. Note, for prose there is nothing in the 'Spacing' boxes 'Before' and 'After' nor the 'Indentation' boxes. Click 'OK'.

This will give you an appropriately formatted prose document. Note however that the headings are no longer how they should be, therefore these will have to be formatted.

4. Alternatively, if you wish a block paragraph style such as might be more suited to poetry or nonfiction, use the 'Paragraph' Dialog Box to format your paragraphs like this, although you might want to use different line spacing. Change the 'Spacing' section to '6pt After'. This gives you a space between paragraphs. Change 'Special' to 'None'. Click 'OK'.

Back to formatting the prose style now. You will see that the title is now sitting in the wrong place, so what we have to do is go back and centre it all, plus put in a page break.

5. Highlight your title and anything else on the title page. In the 'Format' menu, select 'Paragraph' to open the paragraph box. (Do not use the icon to centre the text).

6. Change 'Alignment' to 'Centered'. Change 'Special' to 'None'. Do not forget the 'Special' box otherwise your title will be off centre. Click 'OK'.

Now you need to separate your title from the beginning of your book so we need to put in a page break.

7. Place your cursor on the last return on your title page and then click on 'Insert' in the menu bar. On the drop down menu select 'Break'. Click on 'Page Break', it will probably be selected already. Click 'OK'.

8. Now go through your document and centre headings, chapters or titles in the same way you did your title page. If you have asterisks between scenes, centre them too.

If you want your chapters to start on a new page follow the same instructions for placing a page break as was indicated for the title page. This is for Kindle only. Do not put page breaks between chapters for Smashwords, the meatgrinder (autovetter) does it automatically, provided the word 'Chapter' is in the heading. If you put page breaks in as well it may result in blank pages between chapters.

If you want a page at the end of your book for an author bio, insert a page break at the end and then add the details you want.

If you add other published books and intend to use Smashwords as well as Kindle, they consider themselves the publisher and don't like references to other publishers.

If you add other publisher details or hyperlinks to other publishers, apart from Smashwords, you won't make the Premium collection and therefore won't be distributed to the Apple iBooks store, Barnes and Noble etc. You can, however, refer to your books as being available at all major bookstores as long as names are not mentioned.

If you want extra spaces anywhere in the manuscript do not use paragraph returns to do this. *Smashwords Style Guide* says no more than two paragraph returns should be used to avoid blank pages but in reality, I have found that even one paragraph return can result in a blank page. If you want additional space use the 'Before' and 'After' Spacing fields in the paragraph box, but ensure the maximum space used is no more than 10pts. The only place you should ever use additional paragraph returns is your Title or Copyright page and your additional information page at the end of the book.

And never, ever indent using the space bar or tabs! Do everything through the Paragraph Styling Box.

Adding Metadata

With your document open:-

1. Click 'File' in the menu bar;

2. Click 'Properties' in the drop down menu;

3. Enter title, author name, and keywords;

4. Click 'OK'.

Hints and tips

Indentation: One conversion problem I have noticed that occurs during the process of making a Kindle version of your book is that paragraphs which are not indented have an indent after conversion.

In fiction, the first paragraph does not usually have an indent, although all other paragraphs do. If you don't mind your first paragraph being indented you do not need to do anything. However, if you prefer the non-indented paragraph to remain, there is a workaround and it is quite simple.

Your indented paragraphs will be either 0.3 or 0.5 of an inch or the metric equivalent, so the answer is to apply an indent to the first paragraph as well. This indent should be as small as you can make it so that it is hardly visible to the naked eye, but is recognized as an indent by the conversion process. I usually apply an indent of 0.05 of an inch which is 0.127cms.

Formatting for Kindle checklist

Did you remember:-

1. To turn on your formatting so you can see if there is any rogue formatting remaining – in particular, any tabs and any additional paragraph returns. If any are found, delete them;

2. To get rid of headers, footers and page numbering;

3. To clear all formatting prior to reformatting;

4. To check that all new formatting is based on 'Normal';

5. To centre your title page and copyright page;

6. To centre all chapter headings and any other headings you have;

7. To centre scene dividers or asterisks (if you have them);

8. To put in page breaks between chapters for Kindle only – not Smashwords;

9. To add metadata;

10. To check that the only paragraph returns in your document are those required to start a new paragraph There should be no other paragraph returns anywhere else in your manuscript with the exception of Title, copyright and back pages;

11. To check the ebook in Kindle Previewer before publishing.

Adding a TOC

Type your table of contents at the beginning of the book, preferably after the copyright page.

Working with the headings in your book

1. Highlight the heading in your book where you want to create the link, for example, 'Dedication'. Only highlight the words you need with no extras.

2. Click 'Insert' and then 'Bookmark' In the dialog box which appears, type your heading eg 'dedication' (only type one word with no spaces) and then click 'Add'.

3. Repeat with every heading you wish to include in your TOC. It is important to use only one word with no spaces in the dialog box, for example, if you choose to do Chapter One, name that as c1, or ch1, or chap1 or something similar. Or if you wanted to use the heading of this section you could simply use 'TOC' as your bookmark heading, but just make sure you can identify it with the full heading in your table of contents.

Working with your Table of Contents

1. Go to your table of contents at the front of the book.

2. Highlight the first entry in the table, eg 'Dedication'. It is important to link all of the text in the entry, for example, in a TOC containing the heading of this section you would highlight 'Adding a TOC'.

3. Click 'Insert' and then 'Hyperlink'. In the dialog box which opens, choose 'Place in This Document' which is in the left column. In the table displayed, select the heading that matches the one in your TOC, and then click 'OK'. You now have a live link from your TOC to the relevant place in your book.

4. Continue to link your table of contents in this fashion until every link is made.

5. Test every link by clicking in the TOC and checking that every link leads to the correct page.

Appendix Two

References and Resources

Useful Books

Clarke, Brendan; The IngramSpark Guide to Independent Publishing. 2015. Graphic Arts Books.

Coker, Mark; Smashwords Style Guide; How to Format Your Ebook. 2011. Smashwords.

Gaughran, David; Let's Get Digital: How to Self-Publish, And Why You Should. 2014. Arriba Arriba Books.

Gaughran, David; Let's Get Visible: How to Get Noticed and Sell More Books. 2013. Arriba Arriba Books.

Giammatteo, Jim, and Ross, Orna: How to Choose a Self-Publishing Service 2016: A Writer's Guide from The Alliance of Independent Authors.

Jones, Wendy H; Power Packed Book Marketing: Sell More Books. 2016. Scott and Lawson.

Penn, Joanna; Successful Self-Publishing: How to self-publish and market your book in ebook and print. 2015

Sedwick, Helen; Self-Publisher's Legal Handbook. 2014. Ten Gallon Press.

Software Information

Kindle Create download; https://kdp.amazon.com/en_US/help/topic/GUGQ4WDZ92F73 3GC

Vellum software to create ebooks; https://vellum.pub/

Calibre download; https://calibre-ebook.com/

Sigil download; https://sigil.en.softonic.com/

Amazon Kindle Create Tutorial;
https://kdp.amazon.com/en_US/help/topic/GYVL2CASGU9AC
FVU

How to Use Kindle Create; You Tube Video.
https://www.youtube.com/watch?v=Fvq1M1HsCrE

Joanna Penn's formatting video on Vellum;
https://www.youtube.com/watch?v=idBXslpSemQ

Resources

ALCS (Authors' Licensing and Collecting Society); secondary
royalties income. http://www.alcs.co.uk.

Nielsen ISBN store; where to buy your UK ISBNs.
https://www.nielsenisbnstore.com.

PLR (Public Lending Right); registration site for library loans
income. https://www.plr.uk.com.

Self-publishing Services

Book Printing UK; for reasonable POD printing costs. They
also offer self-publishing packages.
https://www.bookprintinguk.com.

Clays; printer and publisher of paperbacks and ebooks.
https://www.clays.co.uk.

Draft2Digital (D2D); aggregator/publisher of ebooks.
https://www.draft2digital.com.

Feedaread; paperback publisher offering self-publishing
packages. https://www.feedaread.com.

IngramSpark; publisher and distributor of paperbacks and
ebooks. http://www.ingramspark.com.

Kindle Direct Publishing (KDP); the Amazon platform for
publishing print books and ebooks. https://kdp.amazon.com.

Kobo Writing Life; the Kobo platform for publishing ebooks.

https://www.kobo.com/writinglife.

Lulu.com; provider of ebook and paperback publishing services. https://www.lulu.com.

Matador; provider of a range of publishing, marketing, and distribution services to authors for ebooks and paperbacks. http://www.troubador.co.uk/matador.asp.

Nook Press; Barnes and Noble publishing platform for ebooks and paperbacks. https://www.nookpress.com.

Silverwood Books; provider offering three different packages for their self-publishing services which includes ebook and paperback publication. The costs of their packages are available on their website. http://www.silverwoodbooks.co.uk.

Smashwords.com; publisher and aggregator of ebooks. https://www.smashwords.com.

Legal Responsibilities

Legal Deposit Libraries Act 2003; https://www.legislation.gov.uk/ukpga/2003/28/contents.

Agency for the Legal Deposit Libraries address; 21 Marnin Way, Edinburgh EH12 9GD.

Agency for the Legal Deposit Libraries web site; https://www.legaldeposit.org.uk.

The British Library; https://www.bl.uk/legal-deposit.

The British Library Legal deposit; https://www.bl.uk/legal-deposit/about-legal-deposit.

Legal Deposit Office, The British Library, Boston Spa, Wetherby, West Yorkshire. LS23 7BQ.

Useful websites

Absolute Write forum; a useful place to ask questions. http://absolutewrite.com/forums/activity.php.

Guidelines and tips on avoiding Scams: the Critters Workshop;

http://critters.org/c/pubtips.ht.

Preditors and Editors; http://pred-ed.com.

Reedsy.com; useful website with a database of editors and other self-publishing professionals. https://reedsy.com.

SfEP (Society for Editors and Proofreaders); list a directory of editors at http://www.sfep.org.uk/directory.

Writer Beware; lists of vanity publishers and much more. http://www.sfwa.org/other-resources/for-authors/writer-beware.

Professional Associations

Alliance of Independent Authors (ALLi); http://allianceindependentauthors.org.

Society of Authors (SOA); contract vetting and authors' union. http://www.societyofauthors.org.

Appendix Three

About Chris Longmuir

Chris Longmuir is a well-known Scottish writer, and if you listen to her YouTube trailers where she reads the first chapters of her books, in a distinctive Scottish accent, you could be forgiven for thinking she was born and bred in Scotland. But appearances can be deceptive because Chris was born in Wiltshire in the south of England. Admittedly, she fled England at the tender age of two, but this does not give her the excuse to masquerade as a Scot, no matter how much she would like to.

She was a solitary child, painfully shy, and lived most of her childhood within the pages of books. At one stage she even attempted to read her way through the local library. Needless to say, she failed because she had only one lifetime to live. But immersing herself into the imaginary world of books, allowed her to escape from the nitty-gritty of daily life and playground bullies. She made up stories in her head and lived imaginary adventures, but these were never committed to paper because of her belief that she did not have the skill to do this.

Life trundled on. She worked at various jobs and was a shop assistant, office worker, factory worker, and a bus conductress. It was only later that she gained a university degree and became a social worker. But before that happened she got married and lived a comparatively normal life with a doting husband and children, although she didn't quite manage the usual two point five kids.

In the meantime, she continued to devour books and developed an itch to write them. Once she started writing, Chris never stopped. She started to sell short stories and articles and was happy with that for a time. But that damned itch came back to goad her into writing a novel. So, that's what she did.

Chris wrote several novels before her first one was published. It was the usual round of submission and rejection. But along the way she started winning awards, culminating in the biggie – the Dundee International Book Prize, which led to immediate publication. The rest, as they say, is history.

Since then, Chris has published three books in her Dundee Crime Series, three books in a new historical crime series – the Kirsty Campbell Mysteries – and one historical saga. She has also published a nonfiction book, Crime Fiction and the Indie Contribution, and, of course, this nonfiction book, the Nuts and Bolts of Self-Publishing. She has been traditionally published but is now an indie, and proud of it.

Chris has found her forte in crime writing and is never happier than when she is killing off her characters. In fact, her friends joke that she cannot write a shopping list without adding a murder or two. But they also say that she is a very nice lady – honestly, she really is.

Chris continues to scratch her writing itch and is currently writing a new historical crime novel, although there are many more stories rolling around in her head. It's the same problem she met when she decided to read her way through the library – she only has one lifetime!

www.chrislongmuir.co.uk

Also by Chris Longmuir

DUNDEE CRIME SERIES

Night Watcher
Dead Wood
Missing Believed Dead

KIRSTY CAMPBELL MYSTERIES
Devil's Porridge
Death Game
Death of a Doxy

HISTORICAL SAGAS

A Salt Splashed Cradle

NONFICTION

Crime Fiction and the Indie Contribution
Nuts & Bolts of Self-Publishing